FUTURE HISTORY

FUTURE HISTORY

RAJAN P GURUVANSHY

Notion Press

Old No. 38, New No. 6
McNichols Road, Chetpet
Chennai - 600 031

First Published by Notion Press 2017
Copyright © Rajan P Guruvanshy 2017
All Rights Reserved.

ISBN 978-1-946641-22-9

Contents

Foreword

Building is a process. For a strong building, a strong and deep foundation needs to be laid.

We are very familiar with this concept when it is applied to the brick and mortar construction. We are aware that - A Weak foundation is a threat and therefore, we need to take care of it or fix it.

This subject is also true in the case of self and building a family. Somehow, we are yet to pay the desired attention to have a strong foundation when it comes to building the self and one's own family.

Through this book, attempts are made to showcase a few thinking processes. The subject needs to be further studied. In this fast-paced communication media age and with acquired skill, the process of building one's own foundation is better possible through information collation and its effective dissemination. A relook into our personal and family history appears timely - for consolidation and transfer of values to your children, *the next generation*. A culture of knowing your own history, making history and passing on the legacy needs internalization. Otherwise, we are likely to add to the existing stock of us without a history.

Like our urge to attain higher standards of living, universal brotherhood and welfare, a culture of knowing ourselves, our family and neighbourhood will make us better empowered to achieve our common endeavour. It is a mighty social re-engineering process and only you can address for you and for your family.

The essence of the book is designed to enable you to trigger the thinking process, translate it into action and build your own personal history and if possible, your family history. That will ensure your future history.

Episode I

History, History Making and Future History

1.1 History

Papa, What's your Papa's name?

Parameswaran.

His Papa's?

Kannan.

His?

Madevan.

His?

I don't know, son.

Why?

There is no record, available to me,

Why?

Perhaps, our family has only short history!

Or, no recorded history, Papa!

Perhaps, you're right.

Papa, if it's not available, why can't we make our own history?

You mean, Future History!

Whatever you call it! If it's not there, what's wrong in making it?

There's nothing wrong; but you'll be like earlier Raja, Maharajas or rulers. You need power to make history, make

others to record and pay for their service.

No, Papa. Time has changed.

Now most of us are empowered, and the social media is a good carrier to record and disseminate information.

You mean a record of our self, actions, ambitions and of our near & dear and neighbourhood?

Papa, perhaps it is a clean slate to begin with, like myhistory.com. Thereby, a culture favourable for recording our true

history will emerge.

That is a new school of thought. The youth can definitely attempt.

Papa, we need your co-operation, I mean elder's co-operation.

What for?

We need your help to fill the immediate missing links and this could act as a stimulus in to making our History.

It sounds interesting.

Let us make an attempt to probe into our own history. The subject perhaps was earmarked exclusively for history makers. However, it would be better if history is traced by each individual. To live a better and happy life, each one of us must be familiar with the art of history recording and even making our own history. The recording process will inspire us to think and acquire the skill. Slowly, it can emerge as part of our culture, a harbinger of a dynamic culture with the desired changes. It will help us in ourselves, our family, and even in nation-building process.

The existing data/information related to the subject history is more academic in nature. It is shaped by a microscopic minority for those wielding power. If we recognize our worth, we can have our own history. That will trigger the change process as in the case of the desire for good food, loving companion and better living standards. If we want to develop a true history of ourselves, we should do the same. The history currently taught as a subject in classrooms and showcased are of earlier initiators. We may love or hate them. The subject is lively. Let us make use of those platforms as launching pads and find our own roots, record our own history and emerge as history-makers.

The social security, freedom to travel and choose occupation, earn, save, invest and inherit makes the subject better worthy to be well within the change process. It will make us realize our own strength. The roots will enable us to strengthen them and then build. Our dreams can be better realized through the newly created better connectivity. The process of building will be better internalized and the unfortunate gene of destruction dominating due to an unpleasant history can be slowly put to death.

For addressing the social re-engineering process, first we have to accept and recognize the need to have our own history. Then we have to record them based on available information and also encourage family members to contribute. If possible, share them through social media and make it accessible to those interested. The process of probing, realizing and making history will become a part of our culture. Photographs, brief write-ups, paintings, short films, any literature available etc. will help the process. Our yesterday is our history. Today is apt to make history and record. Encourage your friends in joining the thinking and change process. New methods and process will emerge. It can be one of the large change processes. Its' beauty can be its own larger scope for building participatory spirits, knowing ourselves, our own near and dear, the far and wide and to be better inclusive in the emerging global village. Let us initiate the process in India and join the large national program Make in India.

Papa, I have my childhood photographs, videos, certificates received from schools, colleges and my own daily jottings. Can I attempt to record my own history?

You should. It is only a beginning and slowly you will acquire the skill. Based on your perception, the subject can acquire many facets. You record the events of your life. It will be appreciated and better traits internalized by the incoming generation. They will have access to the real history of their own past and not the history drafted under pressure. Those are currently kept in library, museum and they make scope for further explorations and excavations. It was a duty or a business for them and not an internalized culture of you and me. Let it continue; and, you should add on with the new facets. Together you can fill in the historical divide, presently felt. An entry to even history is unfortunately restricted to us, the large majority, the leftover. So break the convention and create your own history.

Papa, like me, the majority of us may not be able to trace more than 3 generations; whereas, a few among us may be able to trace more than 10 generations. Will it not be a disadvantage to us?

Three generations is like 100 years and 10 generations are therefore, 330 years. It is not much when compared to the more than 2 Million years of history, that science supports on our existence on this planet. We all have short history only. Even Vedic period claims to have a backup of 4000 years only. They are drawn up by our own forefathers and retained through the art of memorizing, carving or drawing pictures on rocks, making sculptures and writing on copper plate and palm leaves. During those times, only a selected minority participated in the process. Others were hunting, food gathering, defending, cultivating, migrating, settling, capturing, demolishing, rebuilding, looting, dying, killing, peace-making, fighting for freedom, running democracy, practicing corruption, agitating, punishing, producing goods, trading, rendering services, institution building, cheating others, waging wars, making laws, wielding powers, adding new goods, rendering services, using knowledge, making money and a large majority missing opportunity to enter in the main stream of life. Opportunity to make history was limited to them. They therefore, miss in the present recorded history. Realize the situation and ensure your participation and make others inclusive. A large quantum of energy can be further tapped optimizing the efficiency in deployment of the factors of production. This will lead to wealth creation, in measurable terms which you and I are currently familiar with.

Papa, are you advocating a concept saleable?

Probe into once own roots for our own self-empowerment. Say, history for money making!

Make history.

Make money.

Exciting.

1.2 **History Making**

To begin with, we can start from ourselves. Record events based on our own memory on childhood, school days, the experiments we made during adolescence, our own family members, observations during travel, our dreams and thinking process, the strange happenings we witnessed, those things we heard, read, discussed and deliberated. We can also add our views on our neighbourhood, the system around us, the environment, the society, our involvement, the striking factors we have observed which are in our memory etc. Record anything and everything which one likes. We are the creator and therefore, our own masters. Cultivate and nurture the habit. Slowly, a faculty of our own will enable us to select the best we feel fit. That will constitute the bench mark of our history making faculty.

Extend this attempt, covering your own family members. It will open avenues for self-learning as well as knowing those near and dear. The process will enable you to be more with your family members. It can definitely help better integration within the family and help you to shape them to your liking. Use simple language; better mother tongue or the common dialect your family members use. Perfect the write up adding humour and using audio-video aids. Ensure the participation of your family members. It is worth spending time, money and paying attention. Along with the hero-heroines you admire on your T.V. screen, you also start enjoying the role played by your family, their achievements, mischievous and hilarious activities.

We can, to an extent limit the invasion of others through the cable in to our own privacy. Unfortunately, the present system continues to inject inferiority complex in our mind, especially among our children, adolescents, women and the elders. The cable, similar to the earlier myth has penetrated in our homes. Let us learn to make use of it and make it dance to our tune and to our convenience when time permits. If you are bold, request your cable operators to plug on your audio-video and inculcate a habit to see yourself and improve your performance. It will be better than many serials and box offices you currently tolerate. For business, your cable operator will develop new methods to address the emerging market. Your hobbies, travelogue, picnics, family functions, get together parties, children's initiatives, collective interest, group dynamism, team work for addressing common issues etc. are subjects worth watching and will better go along with the current market *masala*, product-mix. A system for better knowing yourself and enjoying your group living will also find space along with the current market *masala* we tolerate for the last half-a-century.

A perusal of the social media and the nearby libraries will give you a variety of methods in recording the family history. Most of the attempts are made by families having stronger ties and due to an initiator. Of late, I could see a family with a practice of recording history of their elders in wooden planks and hanging the same in veranda. A simple method they could continue for the last 300 years and the wooden planks speaks volumes of their family history for which they are proved of. The culture, they claim to have inherited through Buddhism. During those days the teachers on the move handheld the social living system based on self and family empowerment at village level.

A variety of such practices are still prevalent. It indicates that the system of self-recording and recording the family history was well practiced and it discontinued for some reasons. That subject is beyond the scope of our current perception. Presently, with the availability of cell/smart phones ,evolving *selfies* and social media, anyone can address the subject. Such initiatives will result in larger participation, wide variety of thinking, innovation and methods to strengthen the subject. The new avenue will also enable the majority to realize their Strength, Weakness, Opportunity and Threats and will make them better equipped to participate in the fast changing scenario in the global village.

There are obvious advantages in the social frame work of a family. The very survival of the institution reflects its strength throughout the global village. Keeping their social values, can we professionalize the institution? If felt required, a true history of it is required as a bench mark to address the professionalization process. Or else, the institution will remain back dated while its members will undergo timely updating. The miss-match will lead to institution's expiry date. Symptoms of such value degradation can be seen on footpath, railway platforms, wine shops, temporary shelter on pavements, more unwanted and the less cared. If left unchecked, the global village will add sizable number without history. It is not a welcome change. It is definitely not a concern of the governments. It is a business of both you and me. It must be addressed. Realisation and Internalising of own family as an institution is therefore, warranted. Its framework is human made and it needs updating. Your initiatives on your bench mark will enable history making process at home.

The very awareness on existence of family as an institution needs conscious recognition. Many of our smart managers have family problems. Their managerial skills in cooperate management fail to work at home, may be due to the very lag in time often resulting in identification of family based issues. The subject and related its problems solving systems are currently addressed by a limited number of family councillors. They try to solve mostly personal issues and not family related issues. It needs a different set of treatment or problem solving approach. We currently have no school on achieving better professionalism in our family. The subject needs larger treatment. Your attempts to record your history and history of your family will serve as the basic reference materials for researchers and change agents to establish the familiar R&D on family and develop new professional schools.

Papa, we are in a market driven economy. There is lot of inter-personal and inter-regional inequalities in our access to assets, our skill and managerial talents. Institutionalization or family building in such a scenario appears complex and it will be varied based on the level of acquired assets, knowledge, inherited culture and skill of each family. Whether it is a workable subject?

You have understood the subject. It is a complex one. That is our social system and it is the reality. We learnt the art of survival with constant efforts from surrounding environment and social system. Often we championed ourselves in destroying the efforts made by others and looting their valuables and hoard it up. Along with a skill on creation, we nurture ourselves the skill on destruction. Lot of time and energy is wasted between the process, skill formation, building, demolition and destruction, again acquiring skill and in re-building. The process makes hurdles on our collective quality up-gradation of our living system. A careful understanding of the current social system by you and your neighbourhood will enable us to build ourselves and our family, relatively better.

If we turn the pages of our own recent past, stories on destruction are dominating. History is often recorded more on our attempt to destroy what our brothers made. Similar to the destruction we witness in the case of cities, fort, palaces, factories, markets, shipyards, airports, civil stations, buildings, dams, roads and bridges, we have also destroyed our own skill we acquired even on the art of love making, our compassion to the life system, the faith between and among us, the dependability, the much wanted freedom, social security and mood for creative thinking, experiments and attempts to reach perfection on our services, finished products, market accessibility and affordable prices. Much of the destruction is invisible. But they are larger issues drawing our attention. However, we continue to make only films on destruction. We also display in museums our lost heritage; and we love to see our actions against oppressions in theatres. It is a business and its scope of late, has widened and reached even to our living rooms, facilitated by the remote in our hands.

These are our invisible traits and to realize them, we may have to use our brain. For addressing the issue, first we have to wake up and recognize ourselves. Second, we have to acknowledge ourselves that we have a family and it is an institution and we need its updating. Third, we have to be familiar with our roots; our traceable history. This will enable us to initiate the change process with the objective of building ourselves and our family as an institution. Remember, we are on history making.

Our self-awareness and initiatives will trigger on the building process. We will start loving other builders and even will extend our hands on the re-building process. A variety of success stories will emerge. It will fill our living rooms recharging our T.V. viewers currently confused on destruction and family feuds. It is a large market, yet to be explored. Through the change process, a new set of gene will emerge in our own body; slowly replacing the current accumulated leach like gene on destruction. The language of destruction is easily understood like when someone kicks on your back. Whereas, the art of building is pain staking to realize like the lone boy making a hut on the beach with wet sand. The pleasure on building is to be felt. Currently, we witness more on destruction and the wailing 'Ayyo'; with wide mouth and bulging eyes. Leave the scream and learn to identify the hidden creative talent in you. It is your faculty for building. Never neglect. Presently, it remains mute. That makes us dull and our homes poorly lit.

Unfortunately, we have a liking to witness the suffering of others. We love to sympathize even by beating on our chest. But, we fold our hands, stand staring at an initiator, wait for his fall and sympathize. The faculty of extending our hand to make him success is not in our gene. It has to be brought in and cultured for our own skill up-gradation on building. We have a large army of ourselves to make legislation, for their enforcement and for our own defence, because, we are always worried on destruction. Only a microscopic minority among us are builders. As a result, our faculty on building remains on nascent stage. Majority of us fold hands and wait to witness the destruction. The process is well internalized through religions and through our culture. It needs changes, especially when you are on making history and the history of your family. Majority of us are less conscious on this subject. Therefore, changes are desired. It will ensure your history.

We've a scientific support of 26 Lakh years of our existence. Still majority of us face difficulty to find a decent living or to possess a minimum required accommodation on this vast planet and to fetch even the essentials. The market is in its operational perfection. However, we are confronting a variety of problems for the last 4000 years. There is scarcity of all essentials, especially to the majority. This segment unfortunately has no history or too short history. A relook on the subject is timely. The subject is not market led; and therefore, currently, a free good. We have the basic education and skill to look into ourselves on what is lacking among us. If it is history, this write up attempts to enable you to kindle your thinking process to make history – history of yourself and your family.

1.3 *Future History*

The subject history deals with events of 'our' past. So, future history is something new and it is currently not in our pipe line. Let us collectively make attempts and showcase ourselves in the new bus, the market. I see those missing their history and they constitute a large market. They are an emerging segment on the Global village. The market is vibrant. Let us get into the new global carrier, the new bus and perform. A humble attempt is made on the following write up to showcase a few faculty on which we may like to pay attention on making an entry to the market, making history of ours, and to enable our near and dear to make history of their choice.

For convenience of the readers, the write-up is arranged as episodes as in the familiar TV program at home. Each episode is self-sustaining like our own existence in the family and society. However, each one is inter-linked with the rest. There are a few traits in the vast space of human mind; which is dynamic, subjected to change; and, therefore, requires constant addition and deletion. The writer makes an attempt to initiate the thinking process by handholding the readers to make their own history and to change the present ethic of the majority, missing in history. It is a re-engineering process, for the leftover to be in the emerging history; to be in the bus of the new revolution. We have missed buses earlier. Never repeat the mistake. Board in the new bus and make history. We have to ensure our future history.

Episode 2

Love, Care and Compassion

2.1 Love

All of us love to be loved. A young lady associating with us in a survey work said,

'Sir, I'm unable to reciprocate my love to match with the love my sons aged 6 and 4 express to me. Something is holding me'.

The lady was 26 years of age, smart and good at her work. I thought that we the 'grown up' too have this limitation. Our children too might have acquired our 'quality'. The incident clearly indicates that we are poor in expressing our love.

Love is not a priced commodity. It cannot be hoarded or saved for future use. Still all of us are miserly in expressing our love; even to our beloved like the kids above. If you feel you are Ok, skip this episode. It is meant only for those having a limitation on expressing their love.

The lady perhaps felt a small stock of 'Love' and she is compelled to ration the same as happening in our familiar ration shops supplying inferior quality of the essentials. Or whether it is due to our constant use of inferior quality of all inputs including love which makes us miserly in supply of love and always ensuring inferior quality even in Love?

If we look at ourselves, our family members and our own near and dear, we can find scarcity in production and supply of love. Each one of us wants good quality and plenty of love. From the time of Lord Buddha, we are trying to ensure regular production and judicial supply of the 'item' LOVE. We all are trying each day. But lot remains to be there; undone, unattained.

Shall we look into the subject?

If yes,

Then look to yourself, close your eyes and search your own supply source of LOVE.

If there is scope for loading more love – Load it – Load it to the brim.

Sit there with full of love, like your cell phone is plugged. When totally charged, know it yourself and start loving yourself. You love your own body, your mind, your profession, your day, your own sound, your own smell, your own taste, dreams, feelings, deeds, thought process and smile at yourself.

Realize it.

Realize love and smile yourself.

Love yourself

Realize the mighty love, Almighty has filled in you.

You will bloom with LOVE.

Your eyes will sparkle, lips will be loaded with blood, body full vibrant like the cell phone, you just charged. It will give you a service based on its capacity, few hours, one day or couple of days. Use the entire newly acquired charge on love to love you only. Be miserly. Don't divert love. Love yourself. Smile yourself. Showcase yourself in the market as a precious commodity. Be pleasant. Eat moderately and do exercise. Love yourself. Smile yourself and showcase. Be selfish. Experiment. You are not going to lose anything. It is your own experiment.

What can be the result?

The fool in you will call yourself a fool.

And you will stop the process.

And, you will surrender to the similar around you.

The status quo will continue.

Most of us are wandering on the globe, wanting love.

You may even scream out.

None loves me. I'm left alone. Even my Mom does't want me.

Still you will not love yourself.

The fool within you will never allow you.

That is the culture.

It has to be broken.

And, only you can do it.

Not Lord Buddha, Jesus Christ, Prophet Naby, Guru Nanak or Sree Narayana Guru.

They are only Teachers. They have taught enough.

You have to perform.

Believe in them and perform.

Don't follow the fool in you; the culture taught by vested interests.

After realizing Love and graduating yourself on self-love, if any scope or strength remains within you, you can start loving others. Based on a careful assessment of your stock of love, you prepare a list of persons, near and dear, friends, pets and environment that you would ration out your precious love.

Slowly, you will find yourself that you can stock more love in your godown and along with supply, the stock will get automatically replenished. Unlike the commodity in the market, there is no scarcity of the item in your godown.

You will feel rich.

People love the rich.

They will start loving you more.

Slowly you can be a showman, a hero, without investment and not using your ATM Card.

It is a change process, and one has to internalize.

After enlisting the persons you wanted to love, start loving them like turning on ignition key of your car or kick starting your two-wheeler.

Give them a full smile.

Hold them, if you're permitted.

Share the warmth. Share the news. Share the heart. Express. Your battery will get automatically recharged by the nature. That is the beauty of God's creation.

When you kick start an unused or less used bike, it may take time to respond. Kick them until it starts. You might have observed boys even jumping on the kicker, tilting the vehicle or pushing them to start. When it is started – Ha! Ride on it. It is wonderful. The great teachers are dead and gone.

Presently, we are more used to the items like bikes and cars.

Let us make them our Gurus and learn.

Starting is more important and not the Guru.

While riding the bike, follow traffic rules.

While expressing love, follow social rules.

Be within the rules; also know about the policemen and other road users. Safe driving is important. Similarly, safe loving is also important for the social animal.

Often social policing dries up the faculty of love.

Our social living system is less accommodative.

Our religion is wrongly interpreted by dry persons those missed the faculty of love.

To them, Love is sex. They even don't know that nature has designed sex to a limited period for man and during childhood and old age there is no sex difference. It's more for statistics. These wise men make rules and regulations and they guide us and deny us from all good things in life. They hide things. They create fear and the faculty of love dries up. The poor lady engaged in survey work is made incapable to express her love even to her kids. That is culture. The wrong culture imbibed in each one of us. We are afraid to express our love.

Once an office assistant revealed herself in Mumbai in the apex bank premises, 'Sir, I start breathing when I reach this office. Another 8 hours I'm safe, cared and enjoy; and wait for the next day'. Unfortunately, working places are emerging as better living places compared to our homes. Somehow, we neglected our home and we make our houses less beautiful and aspire for happy living. We parents have a major role in making our homes to shelters. It happened because we grew up with more of a bad culture dominated with hatred, less with love and compassion.

The faculty of love has its own manifestation. Often it is highlighted as the care a baby gets in Mum's holding. A smile, a stroke, a hug, a touch, sparkling eyes, a turn of the neck etc. are a few of our own unaccounted gestures on love. A culture dominated by slavery, perhaps created fear in place of love and checked the above reflections. It needs corrections.

2.2 Care

There is a craze for getting cared. At all stages, we long for the care of someone near to us. The word careless, we are more familiar with than the word care. After crossing infant and childhood stages, we appear to be careless in nurturing our faculty on care due to cultural limitations. However, all of us long to be cared. We had advantage of western mannerism through colonial rule and we love to make their proud exhibitions. But rarely do we practice that culture at home. We are still shy to take care of our near and dear even at home. We mix it with sex and act like careless forgetting our faculty to take care. Like *Kabady-kabady*, the Asiatic game, we create tension on this subject though all our great teachers marketed care and we have a history of more than 3,000 years on the subject. Please take care; it will be handy for you to be in history. First take care of yourself, your family, your neighbourhood and your local environment. Care yourself first; and, take care of others. The faulty, need rejuvenation; especially among those having no history.

Many of us consciously retain our feelings on care in order to please our own doubting loved ones. They doubt your faculty on care because they are afraid of losing your love to them. As a result, in certain society, a mother-in-law is made less capable to love and take care of her daughter-in-law. A husband or wife is unable to love their sister-in-law or brother-in-law. Often, even sons are forced to avoid their own father. Those are interpreted as inherited great and proud culture. Actually, it happens due to ignorance and inbuilt communication gap. Perhaps due to poverty, and induced fear, an inborn threat is often visible in such relations. Urbanization, nuclear family and the modern gadgets like T.V. has reduced their severity. A poor understanding on inherited culture and its blind wrong practices still make us careless to take care of our loved ones. We often live with 'we don't care' attitude. This leads to careful carelessness and even their institutionalization. Many of us practice the wrong concept. Let us change our bad mannerism and take care to care ourselves.

In a large region, in Asia, the young and even women still prefer open toilet neglecting to those built at home by the local govt. and provided to them free of cost. They prefer road sides and make themselves comfortable by standing on their feet and covering their faces from the head lights of passing vehicles. The reason was reported to be that the young cannot sit on a toilet seat which an elder like their father-in-law or mother-in-law sit and use. Such incidents are streaks on the impact of a mighty culture, the region is proud of when they talk on caring elders. Perhaps, in the long-run, such areas will make larger business on tourism, if the practice is continued like heritage and showcased. These are avoidable pretentions under the divine subject care. Internalize a culture to care your youngsters. If we fail to take care of them, what value the on lookers can attribute on their exhibited bottoms?

In T.V. shows, we often hear 'Take care. Take care of yourself'. Those are heard more often by our loving heavy weights, the obese sitting and even lying down in front of the T.V ever munching. Though they are in love with their role models, they never take care of their message. It is also a fun for them. This is our proud culture at home and we have to be more careful if we want to be in history.

There was a time, just 150 years ago, a mighty king in a place called Travancore, in the present Kerala state in South India who taxed on breast. If he were alive, he might have switched over to weight, the body weight, a better quantifiable item for assessment. Take care; such evil genes are still with us. If we fail to take care of ourselves, the powerful will find new scope for taking care of their interest at the cost of our carelessness.

We do not care ourselves; because, we don't have a faculty to take care of ourselves. We are generous to admire a person in good shape. But we miss the gene to fix a full mirror at home and look at our own body. It is a shame for us; as if we do not own it. It is a fact that vital parts are to be discovered. A world famous novelist in South India cooked up a joke on a popular film comedian, a guest at home and a known miser. He gladly parted a few coins to a boy who could discover something like Archimedes and shouted 'I have seen, I have seen,' while the film actor was taking his bath in moonlit night drawing water from the well. The boy could discover something which the comedian was unable to see for himself for past 3 decades. It is a humorous revelation of an unhealthy culture of not caring our own body. Body care is a Trillion Dollar industry today. Don't spend money for getting better shape. You can better save money by eating less and sweating out the accumulated fat by running, jogging, walking, skipping while seeing your favourites in the T.V. You take care of yourself. Realize that the market is dipping their hand in your purse, sucking you through a wire or a dish.

Take care of your possessions. Make them clean, functional and colourful. Non possession is the best possession. Follow our mighty culture first to leave, non-possess the unused. Your table top, cupboard, kitchen, store house and home will be with more space to find user friendly new items of your choice. The market is vibrant on used items both sales and purchase. Make use of the dotcoms and sell those unwanted. Look at your mirror and even at your heart and trim yourself to showcase your real possessions in the global market or, carefully preserve them. Perhaps, the young at home will market them as vintage or heritage or inherited antiques.

The subject is complicated therefore, you be selfish. First take care of yourself and your possessions only. The rest leave to the Gods. They are to be given a space for their performance. You are not a God; and you can't change others. But you can change and take care of yourself. No whistle blowing is required; if unable to address your own changes, find out the exit. Add yourself to the much wanted organic manure, making our mother earth trim and fit. Let us not blame Gods, our fate, the scriptures or the horoscope and find excuses. Own the responsibility of caring you. And, learn from the process how to care others and be in history.

Those powerful were the market operators, once upon a time. Now, they deliver even at home when you use your plastic cards; which needs recharging. Therefore, think on the faculty of Love & Care and innovate methods for their user friendly use, capture the market and recharge your plastic. If you are a non-performer, the market will delete you. If you are a slow performer, you will find yourself more with dotcoms selling used items, including, perhaps yourself. Presently, most of our actions are market led. There is no escape. This is the new religion; the money led market. Take care, never miss the bus as happened earlier. You will continue to remain in the same status, without history.

It is the new carrier and you have to be in and not out. The youth carrying tags call the process globalization. Let us join the process selling our own valued services, love and care and load our plastic.

Can we, the segment having no history make our history using the lessons our earlier teachers have taught us – the mighty tools on Love, Care and Compassion?

Realize the subject. You have a monopoly market on their inheritance. Attribute values and rejuvenate the sleeping genes in you. The hidden genes will again spurt and flourish.

The writer is a student of economics. He is well within the market and tries to sell the book to you for a price. My immediate goal is to sell more copies. But my success will certainly depend on my ability to awaken the mighty genes in you and make use of your inheritance on Love, Care and Compassion, the much wanted services in the global market.

2.3 Compassion

What is Compassion?

Think about Love, Care and the Compassion within you and within your family.

Compassion is nothing but a joint venture of love and care. The traits can be within you, within the family and extended family. In the market led current economy, it can be used as a tool to strike success. At home, one of you initiate. Others take care of the initiator. He is a beginner. He doesn't have the familiar gods or hero's strength, skill and knowledge. He also doesn't have history like you and others within the family. He is the bitter reality with spurting genes on initiating, an entry to the market, the new bus. Compassion in the current market is nothing, but handholding him to get into the market and carry out operations.

Our short history limits us to continue within the well with our Gods, myth, filmy stories we see and hear. We know more stories told by someone. We have less acquired skill. We have also limited faculty to love and take care, especially taking care of our own initiators at home. That faculty is missing or only rarely seen in our gene. Through careful care, we have to culture and develop them. It's our luck that someone at home has the rare gene to initiate. Handhold and make him perform. You will be in history. Your compassion can work wonders.

We all are in our home. But a few only are with the home and especially with the initiators. Often he feels lonely, left out and get killed himself in the process to reach the market and excel. It happens due to lack of compassion at home. It is a setback. Realize it. It continues to happen due to the long alienation of the vast majority from the main stream of economic activities. Now time has changed. You have freedom. Use it to break the earlier chains and love your own near and dear. Take care of them. Support their initiatives. You are not their enemies. He is initiating and experimenting. Try to join the process with compassion, extending all supporting services. A new culture has to be cultivated. Presently, it is missing; and if we are careless and pose ourselves too busy, we are likely to miss the bus. If we miss the bus again, our fall will be to the much deeper gorge, the *Pathalam*, the familiar hell.

Our daughter-in-law leaves the infant at home to attend her job. Take care of the infant by those at home. You have experience. With added love and care, it is compassion. Enjoy the process. The current practice of sailing against the wind, we should quit. The culture is not ours. It is injected in us by the vested interest to make us stagnant and to be slaves. That lead us satisfied with the reserved seat in *Pathalam* and we are unhappy. Get yourself enlightened. Come out of the trap. The very realization and change process is salvation to the much familiar *Swargam*, the paradise you and I were wrongly taught to conquer when we are in hell, the *Pathalam*. Please unlearn; and, step into the market. Take your people with you and climb the ladder, the market with love, care and compassion. You are the Guru in your tiny island. Internalize *Guruism* and forget other 'isms,' like the familiar politics.

I knew a few ladies. After their marriage; they had to live in metro cities within India in raised buildings leaving their ancestral home having large space. Among them, a few preferred to be within the flat, a sort of protest against the metro culture was visible among them. They spent rest of their life in their flat with their kitchen, toilet and viewing the T.V. They never took pain to make use of the opportunities in the city and always found fault with the different system. A few among them even tried to go back to their ancestral home. There also, they found themselves misfit and returned to city flats. They spent rest of their life only gaining body weight and fluctuating B.P. Time swapped them leaving no history even in the heart of the spouse and kids. This book and my efforts are not for such segments. It is to those cross section, who love to make their own history making use of the available opportunity.

Livelihood is more important than love and love making. When crop cultivation in small land holdings became non-viable, it led to migration of Small and Marginal Farmers and Agricultural Labour to potential areas for wage earning. Urbanization opened new avenues for them. Along with school education and skill formation, the process of migration to potential areas got institutionalized. New patterns of settlements, lifestyle, and family based micro-level production, trade and business practices sprung up. Their dependent receiving Money Orders and remittance from abroad made history often at the cost of this migrant labour. This led to a culture to push out the smart at home.

For survival in new places they made unrecorded history. There was less scope for them to make history and more scope on hard work and pressure on pumping the hard earned money to the place of origin. History was made by the recipients including the governments. Stories and success stories were told and even exhibited by recipients, the media and even governments. None bothered on the real plight of the migrants. That remained unrecorded in history, down the dust and rubbles. Many of them waned out from history leaving those trophies at home. Love, care and compassion were alien to them. Their curse makes the recipients mount tension. A few even wished for their death abroad due to reasons best known to them. One would never find any history about them. In a local area we often identify a smart youth and push him out by force or by false tears. I scribble these epithets to divert you from the corrupt practice and make use of them to make your own history.

Most of the recipients fought for the money and made history at home. That filled the market. A different culture cropped in the local area. A set of new breed sprung out in local area with no skill. They jolly well showcased the inherited culture of urchin, looting and deprivation using the market trends. They loved to call themselves corrupt. They felt no shame on the new tag on them. Competition in corruption emerged. Many participated corruption even posing as critic and their new *Dharma or Dharma*. They could ensure themselves alive, in daily Newspapers and T.V. channels. The media used them for their market assigning new history and news values. No need to think. History making and recording were made easy. A scan on these instruments by incoming generation may be forced to record *Kalky* - a Millennium old institutionalization of corruption. Like the British who dug out the Dark Period in Indian sub-continent, an era of corruption, would be excavated by the new generation.

Time will also explore on manifestation of the acquired skill on corruption and its dynamic institutionalization at home and at global market. This will create scope for new schools on rules and regulations and their administrations. In the chaos, we may forget to live with love, care and compassion. Take care of yourself. Don't get into the trap even unknowingly. The corrupt practices will continue unabated. To check them, you and I should be conscious on our history, the majority, the Leftover's history. Presently, we are nowhere in history. But can we make it?

Perhaps we can. The earlier tools like Love, Care and Compassion need a rework out, as muscles are shaped by machos, the heroes on your T.V. Love yourself. Take care and be compassionate at least to your near and dear, and make history, record and get yourself empowered. Conserve your energy. Deploy it carefully on self-empowerment; and, if possible, empowering your loved ones. Make history; history of your own, using tools like Love, Care and Compassion (LCC).

Episode 3

Time, Counting and Cycling

3.1 Time

The present longevity is short. Earlier it was much shorter. Even our own Dark Period was limited to a Millennium. Slavery, colonialism and invasions were short spans compared to our science supported history of 26 lakh years. We have very short time to perform. Realize it. If possible, quantify and schedule. Please do not leave them to the Gods and to those Heaven above. They are not our rulers.

They are the recently created. You are your ruler. Administer your own time. Do not bother others. To make history, we need time and it is currently short. That makes us all 'busy'. Therefore, find time.

What is our stock of time available during our life time for performance? It may be 10 to12 years, if we account a liberal 50 year period, half a century, at our disposal after childhood and adolescent stage. Of which 25 years will be night and the leftover time for the majority, is just 25 years. It is too short a period to make history, especially those who do not have it. Of the available 25 years, we need ¼th of time for personal care and another ¼th for say, family care. Thus, the balance time for performance is roughly 12 to 13 years. To me, it appears too short a period. Therefore, Time Management assumes top priority. To address the very subject, we have to find time; because, it is a new entry to the time schedule of those having no history or short history. And, we are on the process of making our own history. Don't allow any interference. Exhibit a board - trespassers prohibited. It is a private and very personal affair.

Discover the time available to you. Open a book on time management. Enlist your priority and allocate the time in a day for performance. Focus more on performance. Don't allow your mighty mind to waver like the earlier monkey way, repeatedly taught and internalized. Tie the monkey. Efficiently make use of the time to your own prioritized work. You are on the task, history making. Nobody can stop you. Unlearn all you have learnt earlier. Be selfish and start performing. If you are a student, your grades will be higher. If you are a farmer, you will focus more on your farm activities. Shift your occupation if you find it less remunerative. Find sources for supplementary income generation. Be practical. You have less time. If we can't find any activity profitable, leave it and find a new one. That is change for survival. All will give new hopes and a promise. It will remain as a promise during your life time. Life is for performers in the present market. We remember the invaders and those got power due to their success. Your family will also remember you only when you leave some good things behind, for them. Or else, we are with no history; out of range and unaccounted. In a market economy, things are accounted. Therefore, be practical forgetting the unlearnt philosophy.

For us, those having no history or short history, time is also a resource. The 8-hour time available to a businessman is too long a period. He may fly and attend a meeting at 1000 k.m. distance, fly back and sleep on his bed at home. For the majority, those who commute to work, they will end their day much tired. A wage earner, a farmer or a self-employed will have his own constraint. You will have to be your own judge in time allocation and its efficient management.

There is scope for efficient utilization of the available time. Use all possible time saving devices. Use a bicycle, a two wheeler or a public transport to reach the work place. Use cell phone for communication and encourage your team to make use of the time-saving devices. Modernize your kitchen and cloth washing. If you are at a village, there can be a time-lag in making use of these devices. Break the law. Introduce all time-saving devices which you can afford. Extend the facilities to your children and dependent. Time has changed. We have to run to catch them.

Always take care to optimize the efficiency of the equipments you use or deploy. Make use of the concepts on factor efficiency. Presently, we are less conscious on the subject, efficiency. It may be due to the induced fear, inadequate skill and not using our brain. Unknowingly, we cling to the old system. Self-realization and a faculty to change to achieve efficiency in making use of the time. We have to learn. Acquire the skill and internalize the same to make history.

With the newly felt freedom, we even dare to criticize those attempting changes. We still attribute much value on our past; which actually did not exist for us, the majority. We are nowhere in the history. Unknowingly we continue to fish in the dried up pond and pose as proud owners of our heritage. There is nothing there for us, those having no history. All belong to the minority, the shrewd manipulators. They used us to catch even the last fry in the pond and made their history. But, most of us are nowhere in those time related history. As a result, we missed the time and its gains. If you have still doubt, look at the way your own people are spending time. Ask them whether they are enjoying their life?

Unfortunately, those old trends continue. Be aware of the constraint you are living with. The 12 hours day time and 8 working hours available to you and I is different from those available to our own elected leaders we empowered. For them, country's capital or world trade centre is at flying distance. For you it is still bullock cart, the autos, buses, trains, metro rails or even on foot. Based on your purchasing power, money in your pocket, time also extends its efficiency. For the poor and less empowered, time is often short and for the rich, it is extended. For management of time, money is required. So, for us management of time is more difficult with less resource, less money or no money.

Yet we can make history with added skill on time management and efficient use of our own factors of production. Through such process we can break the tag 'less efficient' stamped on us. Never forget the strength in us; the majority and the market in which we all are trapped. There is no scope for escape. Realize the situation and make use of the time and opportunity. Never postpone; join the market and make your history. We the majority are less efficient in finding time and productive utilization of the same. We are tied in traditions and therefore, yet to address the subject. Many of us feel that it is against the prevailing social order. If you are satisfied with your status, please continue. If you are unsatisfied or less satisfied, initiate self-learning and come out from the cocoon. There is no master on earth to handhold you and I. We have to be our own master like the moth; break the cocoon and fly. Like a swarm of bees, infiltrate into the nearby market. Time is short.

3.2 Counting

Counting is simple, one, two, three, four....... But, it is not as simple, you and I think. We have limitation to count. A couple of years back, I was with a group of commerce students and their teachers in a post-graduate college. I gave them a small piece of paper and requested them to close their eyes. I encouraged them to think themselves in deep sleep at home during midnight. Hearing a knock at door, they realize the presence of Goddess of wealth at their door carrying a good number of bags containing currency notes. She asks you to write down the amount you want, the figure only. I requested my audience to visualize and write down the figure; opening their eyes. One of them collected the chits and wrote the highest and lowest figures on the writing board. In an assembly of around 70, the range was from Rs. 500 to Rs. 75 Lakh. The girl who wrote Rs. 500/- said that she wanted to repay the same amount she borrowed from a friend. A faculty member wrote the highest amount Rs. 75 Lakh. He wanted to build a house on the plot he owned; a genuine requirement.

They were honest and simple. But remember that they had basic education in commerce; graduate or post-graduate students and faculty even with doctorate degree. They represented a cross section of the present majority having no history or short history. I again encouraged them to visualize a few of the most successful businessmen in the world realizing the same dreamy situation. Sudden sprang the answer starting from Bill gate, the I.T. world topper. If he were in my audience, what would have been his jotting? May be in Trillion Euro or Dollars, and perhaps, a figure we are unable to even dream.

Most of us have an ability to count. But it varies. It varies along with our capacity to think. It is heard that in India the economist associated with its first few Five Year Plans had an ambition to handhold the tribal living around his university campus when he was Professor and Head there. They hesitated to the changes, the Professor had brought in. He drew the help of an eminent sociologist who stayed with the tribal and learnt that the target group had limitation to count. Their infinite number is 20, the figures they can count using their fingers in their hands and legs or looking at the changes on the moon. They need only Rs.20 or 20 coconuts, 20 cattle heads, 20 days' stock of essential etc. That is the end of their conceivable dream. Similarly, even our commerce students and their teachers have a limitation to count. It remains with us, the majority as a limiting factor to count.

If we have a higher faculty, people around us may even stamp us as greedy. But on emergency, we may resort to even borrow from them, the greedy; the money lender or the rich. Their history also we are familiar with compared to our own history. We help them to make their history. But we have a grudging respect for them. However, they leave a history behind them. But, the borrowers leave no history and often they leave large debt to their children to repay. This has emerged as a culture. Beautiful literature and films are available on the subject. Writers and film makers earned fabulous name, fame and wealth by showcasing the subject. We have paid and enjoyed them. But, the system continues. Inability to count, continues. History repeats. The faculty to count remains still confused among us, the majority with no history. It'as the reality and we need changes to make history.

Some of the entrepreneur's hard work and lifelong earned assets were wreaked by their immediate generation due to their inborn inability to count. We are poor in our arithmetic. Even our professors of mathematics are poor in arithmetic. It is a fact. Many will pose as if they are not greedy and seek shelter under the theory of wantlessness. With this theory, we can't meet the down payment for a loan or pay back the EMI for even a 2-Bhk flat in a decent place. We are money less and thereby value less in a market economy due to our own inability to count. The subject is a serious one, and we are yet to pay it, due attention. We are yet to recognize and institutionalize the advantage on counting system. We the majority, have poor opinion on the practicing Charted Accountants. Those guys play with figures. So, we have our own inbuilt uneasiness in dealing with them. It's a limiting factor and not fit for those wanting to make history in a market led economy.

Recently, a family friend having an inherited bakery at a business spot in state's capital said he often borrows at 3 per cent from private financers. Later, I understood that it was monthly interest and not yearly interest as I have learnt from banks. I failed to convince him about the working capital credit facilities available from a nearby bank. I have also failed to convince him that he can have such regular arrangements by paying less than half of the current rate of interest he pays to private lenders. It is bondage, and it continues. Somehow, we are unable to make advantage of the added facilities. We could't master the simple arithmetic for our daily life. There are exceptions and those who use the faculty and avoid the common mistakes are history makers. Their success stories are also often shown in visuals and reflected in literature. We often laugh at them. But they are in history. In difficult times, we depend on them and pass comments like that the guy knows the Art of Living; he is a *Kalky Avathar* - fit for 21 century, etc.

Still we will not attempt to improve our counting ability. We have hesitations to open up the faculty. But, we love to be in history without counting ability. It is impossible. If you want to make your own history, you have to strengthen your counting ability. It's a genetic limitation; and, we have to come out of it, for market operations and to make our history.

3.3 Cycling

We are familiar with bicycle. It is a simple device used to go ahead. In circus rings, it is also used for entertainment even cycling backwards. In our life, those segment having no history or less history, cycling means going forward and often reaching backward much quicker, taking less or no time. It is accepted, theorized and institutionalized. Elders said,

Beggars' son will be thrift,

Thrifts' son, will be rich.

Richs' son a spendthrift, and

A Spendthrifts' son, a beggar.

Applicable for the majority, in which you and I belong to. For history makers, the theory is different; and, it is not for us. We are happy or should be happy with the cycle and cycling. We should be law abiding and nature friendly. We are part of the environment. We are a set with no history; and, even hesitant to make history. We are a set, untouched with time and its countable ticks. We are proud to be nature friendly. It is routine like sun rise and it sets. The mighty Himalaya's dynamics we too adopt to be stagnant with its deep roots, soil and worms; cycle and recycle. Worms don't have history. They are designed to carry out the task allotted by the nature. They change the shape of other things. They even shape mother earth through cycling and get ourselves recycled.

But how long it can continue? You and I should decide. Stop the traditional cycling. Be like a modern bicycle rider on street, unlike those in circus rings; which is for entertainment. Why thrift's son should be spendthrift? He should know the value of thrift, savings and investment. It is time to make history. Spendthrifts are currently jokers; whereas investors are on history making.

For a moment, stop your cycling. Stop it and think whether you are on the beaten track. If so, jump out.

Relax under a shadow. The paths on which you cycle are not designed by you and your forefathers. There was a compulsion to all of us, the majority to be in the beaten track. Now it is liberalization. Our earlier thoughts and even our family members were used to the earlier track. They will put you again on the known track and push you to cycle to get recycled. On the course, you can't make history of your own. You will continue to make history for others as can be observed in world wonders. Those monuments are better known in the name of history makers. Where you can find your forefathers who really made them? They remain as a part of environment. When celebrities visit, a few seconds they pretext to remember the spirits on fear due to their likely haunt. They are clever and with silent gestures they guard themselves.

A self-search on our cycling is essential to emerge as history makers. Attempt a self-analysis in your note book or computer. Observe the status of your cycling and your family members. If there is scope for addressing changes, realize the same and cycle to make history of your own. Never cycle to get recycled, like garbage. All of us are in a well-designed trap. Be aware of the choke grip. That itself is the first step to bring in desired changes for you and your family members. Our consciousness on Time and Counting will make us cycle smarter and emerge as History makers.

If you find yourself immature to address the subject, wait and watch others attempting the same. You will enjoy and the tide will carry you too near to the victory stand. Watch the spark on winners and perch on your cycle before you get yourself recycled.

Episode 4

Creation, Continuation and Consumption

4.1 Creation

Creation, in this context has the limited meaning of creating, producing agricultural goods, manufactured products and the variety of services you render. It does not mean reproduction and the blessings of Gods up in heaven.

We are common people with practically nil history and we produce the essentials, anything visible around us and hand over them to history makers. We are no doubt, creators, but less godly. Earlier, we made shelters even to protect Gods. And of late, a few of us make shelters for a large cross section and market them. But, we are yet to make history. We are like that. But, now we don't want to remain like that. We too want to be in the history. The write up is only for them, those who like to make one and a memorable one. We love to have a switch over from the current status of 'no history' to history makers; makers of our own future history.

The target group, with no history are also creators. But they are yet to be noticed or recorded and appreciated. It is a subject, and it is time for us to address. Let us focus on our ability or skill to create. We produce all food grains, pulses, vegetable, fruits and their value added products. We also produce all dairy, fish and meat products and make available to the market and even at the kitchen. We are the creators, the producers and suppliers of all essentials. We also build and transfer the infrastructure like houses, roads, railway, electricity, transport, the chapel, the hospital, the jail, the fort, the port, the parliament house, assembly houses etc. and handover to the minority with history. We are engaged almost in all services, even servicing the Gods closeted all through the globe. We also extend the services to God men and God women. We love and serve history makers. Our produce, products and services are always available to make history. But, we are nowhere in the History. Our role is yet to be recorded. Let us realize the fact and break the culture.

We are to be conscious that we are the creators. The skill is with us. It is worth recognizing, appreciating and transferring.

This can be done without incurring any cost. You need not wait for any one's permission. A self-appreciation of your creativity will spurt the hidden energy within you. Realize it, and make your own near and dear to realize the same. It will trigger the process of future history.

Make attempts to write down the details of the creative ability of yourselves and your family. Encourage your own people to address the subject. A variety of hidden facts on the subject creativity will emerge. Our T.V. programs will have wider scope on the emerging subjects. Knowing yourself and your talent on creativity is a probe on history. We can have millions of recordings on say, wheat production, production of any item etc. and share the information through social media. It will emerge as the largest effort on making history; say, wheat production. Some of the methods will be worth emulating and you will emerge as the real history maker. Contrary to the current history recording a shift on the focus of the subject will find new pastures to perform. It has to emerge in a civilized society. History cannot continue as a subject of barbarians, and, it is not a record on mere dates, months, year and selected events of the vested interest, the minority, the power wielders. Majority of us can also have history. If it is not available, we are to be capable to make our own future history. I request you to bring in the desired changes.

We should record on our talents, it's up-gradation, wealth creation, contribution, efficiency, market intervention, movement of men, material and services. It should evolve as a culture. We should avoid the present practice of paying attention on negative aspects in our society like stories of breaking families, highlighting personal, social & regional weakness and taboos. The process of recording history at personal and family level on the use of the factors of production and its efficiency will self-empower all of us, the history makers, to deploy them with optimum efficiency. Presently, mostly from the minority, management emerges. It has obvious limitations. Our farms and enterprises want professional management. It should emerge from you, the majority. Most of the Grama Panchayat in India, the grass root level of democracy, presently has a dismal picture. As a result, the newly elected ward members look at the sky for guidance. Their available documents so far made are on accounting, to avoid corruption, the familiar subject. Our planners are yet to look into the locally available natural resources and manpower skill and to deploy them for development of local area. History of the local area continues to remain as a virgin subject. As a result, local leadership is yet to emerge. There is scope for future history on this subject. It should emerge from you, the majority. Make use of the opportunity and ensure your future history. There is no need for you to run away from local area. It's a mistake. By doing so, you are not in history. Your dependents will make use of you to make their history. It's happening presently.

Our present schools on enterprises need our handholding to make them effective. They lag in history. The management and faculty are to be forcefully fed on history. Your acquired skill on managing your affairs and making use of them to produce the best, need acceptance and wider replication of the success stories. To optimize production of wheat in a local area, now we turn the pages of books written by the unknown and find ourselves in trouble. This happens in the absence of local history, and due to the lack of culture to record and probe them. We spend a lot in R&D and waste our time and scarce resource. We can guide and handhold ourselves with exposure to our own success stories. Unfortunately, we currently hide them; often due to sheer ignorance and our inherent shyness. We ourselves have a poor value on our own creative ability. It's a genetic limitation. Our managers have more active genes on this limitation. We are in fast changing market economy. Without losing time, we should address corrective measures.

We as creators have 26 Lakh years acquired gene in us. That is a precious resource in us and it can be further perfected by recognizing our own creative ability. Make attempts and realize, first by you. It is possible for you. But, it has to be consciously invoked, like you scratch the match stick. It needs scratching to spurt and light. Make yourself realize the spurting process. Then nurse them. Value your own skill on creativity. In the recent past, your gene remained unrecognized. But it is there and you fully own them.

Many of us even look down on our creative ability. We were wrongly led to look for more, outside. As a result, our skill on creativity has weakened, instead of the much required strengthening. The process made us temporarily weak. A farmer supposed to feed, get himself killed. A goldsmith switches over to lift operator on reasons like social security. Our plight to live, force us to shift occupation. This makes us weaker. When the price of gold and showcasing ornaments picked up in the market, goldsmith who switched over to lift operator had to settle in an urban slum as the lift was available only in urban areas. Holding his kid, he could only peep to the sky scrapers through the rupture of his burrow. The farmer turned head load worker use his head to carry loads with the hidden genes in it on better farm practices and entrepreneurial skill acquired over centuries. Like village deity, he too is scared of the new machines to uproot him from the encroachment. New trends on termination settle: from farmers to head load workers and goldsmith to lift operator. We are on market led natural expunging. Take care and make use of your creative ability; and, make your history in local area. Don't run away leaving your resources, skill and social contact. It leads to physical termination from history.

The minority wrote stories on migration, forced migration, problems of slums, issues they create on civic life, created fear on driving them away, patriotic fervour on local area for local people, policing and patronizing votes. Each day a large army added to the ever swelling size even in new places without history. Within their own planet, they became aliens. Stories were made and sold. Governments were formed and time passed leaving stray records on corruption in the dusty record rooms of judiciary. New migrants searched for smaller burrows and stared at the growing sky scrapers. They forgot their roots and their skill on creativity. Those who left their roots mostly lost themselves and their own acquired skill. A few dons and fewer performers made history while the large majority lost even their identity. The local resources remained idle when her loving creators left her in lurch and chose the urban slums forgetting their creativity. In all urban pockets they were dragged to death without history. Like the earlier *Mahabali* who was driven to the hell for his good deeds, history repeats for the majority. We are forced to attain salvation at urban conglomeration, like our widows at Benares or the migrating Salmon fish. Let us desist from this practice. Can we handhold your friends to make history, using our own Dhama, love, care and compassion?

4.2 Continuation

Sharpening the skill on creativity also needs continuation. Through continuation the faculty on creativity can be perfected through up-gradation of both the skill and technology. The process is best when practiced voluntary based on aptitude. Abrupt shifting of occupation is due to ignorance or compulsion. A relook on our achievements and available history on them will reveal the internal instinct, aptitude and skill for perfection. Genetic gift on our certain qualities are similar to the visible acquired good physical features. In-depth studies on this subject will enhance our own urge for their continuity. Fishermen are a classical example. With modern education, technology and better access to improved varied opportunity available for occupational choice, a sizable majority of fishermen still love to continue in their traditional profession. Economic empowerment achieved by their women is relatively better when compared to those depended on other traditional occupations. Among traditional activities like animal rearing, farming, non-farm activities like handloom and handicraft, fishermen are better focused on their traditional occupation and they are making history with timely adoption of the market led changes.

In spite of the availability of improved technology under crop production, uneconomic size of land holdings make farm activities still drudgery and the high risk prone. This makes farming less attractive. Farmers as a community are proving less successful in building the desired team spirit and making their farm sizable to adapt appropriate technology, farm mechanization and in addressing economies of scale. Fragmentation of land is more in farmers mind and on their boundaries and papers. Lack of team building makes them belly up and leave the land barren and migrate to urban slums. The villain is their own mind and their inability to optimize farm productivity and market their produce and value added products directly to consumers. The media blame traders and middlemen having a larger share on the fruits of farmers sweat. Governments also shake their green horns as a threat on the worsening situation. Those segments constitute the minority with history. Farmers' constituting the large majority is on the run even in a democracy. They run and rub out their own history. A few of them even commit suicide to reach heaven as if in hurry to make history. But, that is not history. Let us realize our own mistake and address our own issues. Never pass our problems to the minority. They will continue to use us to make their history. Both migration and their termination at urban slums are nature friendly; and it should continue. They produce high bred seeds worth sowing in the field of poli-tricks and reaping rich dividends.

Both leadership and media make business on our real script and make their history. The traditional food producers get extinct without history. The land is there as usual. We only shrunk it to the size of a post stamp . Let us realize and undo the stamp size. That will ensure farmers to be in history. Dependents on handloom and handicraft also follow their elder brother, the farmer. They too have no history. Together, they constitute the rural majority, without history. They are more emotional and hesitate to make use of their brain to address efficiency in production, value addition and marketing. Some among them leave their local area and march to conquer the urban pockets and get mostly extinct. They also add confusion and create resentment among the urban settlers. Of late, that too is a political business, and the powerful, the minority use the new avenue to make their political history.

None can check the process, except the affected. Those under traditional sectors like crop production, dairy, fishing, poultry, handloom, handicraft, village and cottage industries, micro enterprises and self-employment should learn to love your own activity, excel in your skill and make your own history. Farmer's children hate farming. Parents hesitate to teach them basic lessons on farming. These results in non-continuation, shift in occupation and neglect of the productive resources. Beautiful terms like uneconomic land holdings, inadequate irrigation, pest attack, deteriorating soil fertility, absentee landlords etc., are used by the minority posing intellectuals and continue to drive farmers away from farming and craftsmen away from their traditional craft. Media encourage the process, highlighting their so called newsworthy news. Governments spend scarce resources on Development Corporations and specialized agencies with their own selected champions to head such institutions. They continue sucking the majority without history. As a result, the locally available resources remain neglected and their dependence get extinct. History, thus repeats. Please realize the gimmick and you ward yourself from further fall.

The majority due to non-continuation lose their prime productive resources like land, labour and managerial skill. In spite of the availability of better farm inputs, electricity and mechanization, farmers as a lot is unable to address farm productivity due to their own culture, the great love for their own timidity, proud customs and practices.

Our farm lands are made stamp size by us only. If I can't address my own issue, who will work to feed my wife? Fragmentation is endorsed by us, the farmers, and none other than you can change your history. When you fail to make use of the land it will be bought by the rich and the governments for corporate level farming, and other business which you could have done, if you had the skill and knowledge to realize your own strength. You are on extinct due to your own time-lag in initiating. In the emerging market, you are submitting yourself unknowingly to be sucked. It is a bitter fact and please, realize. But realize. The writer too was born in a farm family and got sucked. It's our own financial death history. Take care, if you are still alive as a farmer or farmers' son or daughter. Most of the earlier known Small and Marginal Farmers are currently less traceable. Perhaps, they are on the process of extinction without history.

The village level feudal farming was nothing but the present corporate level agri business advocated by the governments targeting the farmers as a whole. Make use of the opportunity, gain strength at your level and make profit as a farmer. It's not a sin. It's a *Punya*, a virtue. Farmers children educated in agricultural schools, colleges and universities are to be retained in farm based enterprises. Parents currently misguide them and even force them to take up clerical jobs in Govt. They look down to their profession. Society lures them to wear ironed cloth, acquire petty power and practice corruption for easy money. Our own hesitancy to address change process at farm level make us worthless and we are forced to look elsewhere to earn the growing needs of our young generation. This becomes the new art of living. They learn new techniques on this and practice. But, they also loose what their forefathers learnt over centuries as farmers. This happens due to low value we assign to our own occupation and not adapting farm based changes like economies of scale, timely technology up-gradation and accessing wider markets. As a result, poor agricultural productivity leads to poverty, poor showcasing of our produces and agricultural labour. We are yet to make history through farming.

The powerful project our failure including the new suicide trends and make their history, make money and flourish in the market. Collectively, the minority wielding power still practice un-touchability and that result in selling our assets and forcing ourselves on occupational changes, migration and suicides. How long our tragic stories will be in our memory through the current media and memories are a subject for research students in future tracing farms and farmer's history and their likely extinction. The large segment are cleverly trapped under market through democracy by entrusting the stamp or power in their figure to press the button and choose their favourite leaders who have already converted to the minority, the powerful, in partnership to share the booty from their operational area using power, making money to ensure their own history. The cult, of late, has become a ritual like the largest assembly during *Kumbamela* or earlier sacrifice or *Guruthy*, in history. History goes on repeating. Take care of your neck. That will minimize the risk in our history making. Try to make a relook on continuation. It should never be a blind continuation. It should be timely up-gradation of the acquired skill, knowledge, technology and market and to be within the market with better performance. Discontinuation is up-rooting. We, the history makers should think twice before our discontinuation.

Feudal and caste system often hesitated to address change. It became a subject for commercial films and they made both history and money. In a few parts of the globe, film actors took the role of political leaders due to their better reach to the masses under democracy and through the media. The newly emerged leaders however, lacked the skill to help the majority to address efficiency and make history. The media too was better familiar with products like stunt, sex, crime and punishment. Crop failure, lack of irrigation, stagnant wages, uneconomic holdings, lack of mechanization & storage, distress sale, avoidable intermediaries etc. remained academic subjects in a community in which the majority was unable to read, write and think. They could play only limited role in rural history. Film actors and musicians could charm them like *avathars*, incarnation, in mythology and make their own history. The vast rural flock remained out of range, the unreached and so far uncovered with proud showcasing the bitter truth by the powerful and making money and using this segment for making their history. These people left their profession and thereby forced to neglect factors of production, manpower efficiency in optimizing production and market intervention. There occurred a great break in continuity. Youth from rural area after acquiring education in urban area continued there even after their studies. Those settled abroad, contributed there, in the host country, and a few made success stories. While they made history in the new land, we lost history makers at our local areas and the benefit through them. As a result of the discontinuity, a new set of people emerged in the leftover places – they are mostly consumers.

4.3 Consumers

The market creates consumers. Technology is used to woo and make them reach the market. A variety of new goods, commodities and services are showcased to lure them in the market. As usual, history makers play their larger role and get further empowered. They even could sweep out the earlier minor producers under the emerging tag of globalization and liberalization. The media support those who pay. For survival, they too are forced to tune themselves under new market operations. Small farmers and small producers were further weakened by the media highlighting their primitive way of production, inferior quality and unhygienic system of production and inefficient distribution. World beauties and celebrities are used to project even bottled soft drinks degrading the local products. The process becomes viral. It accelerated the closing ceremony of tiny units with no history.

Each day thousands of small producers are forced to forget their short history and driven to the larger set of unarmed consumers. In the new bus, it has become a ritual. Elected representatives and the media further firm up the process. The new trend setters unknowingly make history by killing their own budding producers and feeding them to the new sharks. For survival, many scum down to salesmen or distributors. In place of earlier physical trapping of free men as slaves, now the new trap is cleverly used to forget your history as a small producer. A steady termination is in progress. Our freedom to sustain as a producer is clipped through market mechanism. And, our leaders are used to chop off our wings so that we are unable to fly in the market, in the new bus on fast run. This increases our risk factor to be in history. Even at top most leadership level new clippers are cleverly planted to carry out their business. They even exhibit their helplessness due to lack of history in their statesmanship. We all are at a losing stage due to our own lack of history in administering ourselves. We still look at aliens for wisdom; and, they use us. We the majority, again miss our chance to be in history even in a democracy.

New styles on consumerism penetrate each corner in the name of modernization. The earlier producers like farmers, weavers, artisans, and the petty traders are becoming part of history. Their produce and products leave way to larger producers. Tomatoes get rotten near the market places while tomato seeds tagged under high breed loot farmers and killing indigenous varieties. Local seeds, indigenous cattle breeds and fresh water fish which had long history are becoming things of the past. Under paddy itself, we had 800 varieties of seeds and presently we are satisfied with half-a-dozen varieties of paddy. Others are reduced to seed collection banks, that too due to the courtesy of a few scientists. A great sweep down the carpet of the local area's produce, products and skill occur under the new consumerism and through its wide spread advertisement and blind acceptance. The majority with no history may face larger casualty in the elimination trends. A reverse process, a counter action is history making and it should emerge. The mission envisaged through this write up is to make use of the new technology and its wider market reach in making your history, its dissemination and institutionalization.

It is a rejuvenating process and definitely not swimming against the current. The spread of the new market mechanism can be used for recording your history and showcasing them in the emerging global village. In the great sweep, we should have a catch like the floating log, God sent, to the drowning. man Record your history, your local area history, history on your skill, quality, specialization, standards and uniqueness of your produce, products and services. Attribute values on them. Make them worth showcasing. Enlist all marketable items. Make a record, a history of all of them. Use brain, brawn and the new connectivity to penetrate the market. In each local area, there are a few familiar with the market and its access. There are captions of e-trade and e-commerce and through smart phones make link with them. Join the market and make history of your own. Or else, like the indigenous seeds, we too will find our specimen in emerging museums for trading and the rear for viewing. The electronic gadgets are to be used for wealth creation. Presently, it is used mostly for entertainment. In the process, as earlier, we the majority are made into jokers and our women obese. How many hours in a day you want to be entertained especially on others earning? Think and change; so that our kids are not pushed in the world market, empty handed. During my childhood, such situations created urchins. It was common just fifty years back.

I'm writing these notes sitting at Mumbai, a cosmopolitan city and staying at Colaba, near Gate Way of India, where the British developed and established a sea port, their Navy and other military establishments. The heritage hotel Tajmahal, adjoining Taj Tower and the RBI (Reserve Bank of India) Tower where I was interviewed in 1978 as a candidate for their selection as an economist, I can view them sitting at Flat No. 17 in Akash Building of Navy Officers Quarter at Sa-soon Dock. There are so many structures claiming history. A few more towers are also coming up in new markets claiming space in history. So far, I could not make any history of my own. Perhaps, through this writing, I make an attempt to be in the market. I am retired, and carry a stamp on my expiry date. However, You are young and energetic. The market is before you and you are familiar with it. Never miss the bus. Our forefathers missed and we suffered for 1000 years. That is our history. Always remember the roots and board the bus and capture your seat. That is globalization. Also, take care of yourself; or else the market can use you as a consumer sucking the last coin left in your pocket.

Join the market by marketing your produce, products, services and skill. It is history making. You need not be on a horse and a rider like Gengish Khan. Use your brain, computer, social media, your friends, find time and penetrate in market. Use the market for your invasion. Be innovative in locating saleability in and around you. It is market dynmics and you are familiar with this subject for last 4000 years. Your genes have acquired qualities. You and I once produced, traded and exported. You have to rub on your gene and break your own cocoon and fly. You will find yourself in the market. Use the present career as your chariot and explore scope for supplementary income generation and conquer the market and make history. Wage the new market related wars and recording winning calls from your own inner conch.

Be selfish in projecting yourself and your local products, skill, people and environment. There is enough space in the market to perch your tents and showcase. The market is always on its infant stage. It can absorb anything new and even old items. There is no need for encroachment and quarrel. Earlier, most of the fights were for looting. Now the fight is to appease and woo the market, the consumers, mostly our own tribe.

Even if you perish in your efforts to be with the market, it will build basic market related liaison and structure for your children and dependents. They will start with a better platform to play with the market. It will empower them to make their history in their market. Compared to the non-performers, folding hands and observing market behaviours, you will float on the market, finding new operational traits, acquiring skill and performing. You will leave land marks for your near and dear in their market exploration.

The colonialist explored sea routes for a couple of centuries to reach their destinations. That is in history. For thousands of years, our predecessors were on the move to find better pastures, farming land and acquiring them to create wealth. The process resulted in great civilizations, Gods, wars, forts, their demolitions, discoveries, inventions, new skills and their up-gradation. All of this is still taught to us. And, we also have seasoned gene in our body. But so far, none encouraged us to make our own history. History is a subject currently reserved. It is still for the powerful. Acquire power through market and make your own history. Make others consumers; just reverse the procedure. The process itself has large market potential for innovative service providers. Create your own market and consumers. That will create your rich history.

To survive and make history, of late, we have to learn to be market friendly. By buying we can't make history. History is for sellers. As a seller, you can be a better buyer. More selling and less buying should be the dictum for history makers. We, the majority enjoy buying things. Art of selling is less known to us. We spent more time on enabling others to sell their products. We do not attempt to sell ourselves and our products and skill. We have a great shy on the subject. We do not like to market ourselves. On negative marketing, we have specialization. We spread ill of our own near and dear, the known. The unknown don't exist and therefore, we leave them. They are out of range and therefore, have freedom from us. So, they sell under liberal market and we fools buy from them and they make history and we mourn ourselves on our sad demise without history.

For marketing ourselves, we have to love ourselves, our produce, products and services. To develop love on them, it should be worth showcasing. It is possible only through added efforts. We are lazy and shy. It is inborn and carefully implanted and nurtured. Amidst surrounding freedom, we are still tagged like slaves. In ignorance, we continue to tie our own loved, near and dear, because they are reachable and tolerant. Others will kick. So, we focus on our own people and their products and do negative marketing, degrading the qualities and stamping with the familiar ignorance, often quoting from the newly accessed scraps from scriptures. We have champions on negative marketing. They are within us, at home, our religious places, our neighbourhood and work places. Smile at them, and ward off those traditional consumers with no money, if you're on history making.

We all love shopping, especially our women. Shopping with money creates tension and with empty purse, it is fashionable.

We get easy company for both. It is in our gene and we claim extra skills. What about selling? Do we like to market or sell ourselves; or, our own products and skill? I grew up observing families spending sizably long time marketing films and actors. Today, we have even film fans associations to market our favourite actors; and, it is institutionalized. In most of the societies and even in families, there is great shyness on self-marketing. This can be observed even in your home. We don't like to market even our best marketable items. The inherent shyness appears as survival symptoms from the powerful, who could successfully re-engineer our genes to their liking.

While, people belonging to the new faith are proud to display, others are observed hesitant and some of them even hide their identity. I'm looking at the practice and not the merit. The practice reflects confidence. Majority of us, with short history, or forced forgotten history, somehow are less capable to market ourselves. But, we could often trace out the marketing skill in our genes. And, somehow we prefer to use it for others, those having history. We fail to market ourselves, our products, our family members and their quality and achievements. To me, it appears as a bad market trait. This need changes for making history.

The skill currently observed in team building for shopping and enjoying, is missing in marketing our own produce, products and skill. Often, initiatives taken up by a family member is not supported by his own near and dear. In the Art of Living on which we often claim as masters, I'm yet to see team building and handholding to empower the initiators. We hand-fold ourselves and wait to see our initiator's much familiar failure. At his back, we love to talk on his failure. With the same energy, we could have supported him. At an elderly age, the writer too observes the same from his own loving near and dear. It is a great limitation within us, the majority having no history. We don't allow our own near and dear to make history. It is within our genes. Observe and take care of this limitation to make history. New technique to use this hostile segment as your prospective consumers is really an art. If you are successful, your future history becomes colourful.

Be in the market, not as consumers but as sellers, history makers. In the new market we can play our role in it. If we are hesitant, we will die without history, like our forefathers who were stamped under mud in those battles and endless farms, in the process of making history for the empowered. The same practice, somehow we still continue in the new malls where often you find yourself missing amidst the crowd; enjoying pop & modern music, tilting your hips, jerking your joints and often replicating the earlier war cry. We were stamped to death earlier. Now the process is on progress emptying our purse. There is no escape. We have to be within the market. It's the new social order. Join the market selling your items. Support your own market initiators. Handhold them and make history, for survival of your family and to celebrate. Through higher consumption, we lose our money and gain body weight. On selling, we make ourselves fit, firm, smart and beautiful. Then life become worth living and showcasing your real assets. Tighten your belt, sell your products and be trim and make future history for your own incoming generations. But always enjoy your life in the process of making history and be a role model with fewer liabilities and more assets worth showcasing. Use the market and illuminate your life. It's possible for you. Because, I observe those quality genes in you. Realize your own lost history and compensate with bright future history.

Episode 5

Shyness, Complex and Culture

5.1 Shyness

Most of us are shy. We live in shyness. Often, we are shy to even look at us in a full mirror. Our shyness work as a dislike often on ourselves; and, we are forced to look down ourselves. The secret appears logical; there is nothing worth seeing. So, we look more at others, wrapping ourselves in shyness and often institutionalizing the same. We appreciate their trim shape and those larger achievements and celebrity status. We also spend time to project our thoughts on our favourites. But, we hesitate to shape ourselves, observe at the mirror and if possible, showcase at least before our lovers. We don't care. We are great and we care others. Caring ourselves, oh no, it is not in our culture. We may even quote from our limited memory on our traditions and justify our own culture, on the inherent shyness. During my college days, a film actress walked on Mumbai crowded beach recharging the majority's weakened batteries on shyness wasting no money on her cloth. She became a celebrity and I too endorse her history even at this wrong age. We are too good in recording history of even misers who hesitate to buy even bikinis.

There are varieties of shyness. A careful look at the trait will be both humorous and commercial. In its very crude form a visible divide on shyness can be observed between the two sex. Females carry a visible hallmark on shyness than the males. Males of my age adored them when wrapped in shyness. It was considered a virtue in our school of thoughts. Shyness was beautiful in our days. For us it reflected traits of hidden submission, and, we loved it. Literature on the subject can be traced even during ancient period. Shyness was well captured by poets, painters and sculptors during the past. It is even marketed currently as sculptures, paintings, in films, serials and ads. Shyness is a subject worth selling. So we love shyness; especially female shyness.

Of late, social police make new citadels to guard such schools and even fight against the normal police, widening the scope for law based business and practitioners. We are all in the market drawing advantages on shyness. Majority of us enable the process, the smooth market operations on female shyness. Only a few, break the laws of shyness and make their life better lived. They can be called history makers. In the recent past, a young girl in my family broke through her shyness. She got into govt. service, retired after 32 years, drew pension for 36 long years, made history and died. Her two sisters with comparable school education and better appearance spent most of the time at home and departed much earlier, doing no harm to any and not making even a scratch on pages of history. They were shy and traditional. Whether they were able to enjoy their life without earning themselves is a subject for search. As a student of economics, I realize the importance of money. An art of living without money is beyond my perception. I'm perhaps biased. You nurse your valuable shyness. I have no objection in retaining her with you. But, it should never be allowed to curtail your freedom and to make you shy away from realities of our life and your efforts on history making. It is dangerous. Earlier it was considered as a sin and a dereliction from our duty. For *Moksha*, salvation we were allowed a few *Janmas*, rebirth. Now time has changed and in the market there is enough space for youth to perform. There is no need to wait for the long awaited *Punar Janmas*, born again. Currently, decisions are made with money, Euro, Dollar, Yen, Rupee and their convertible. Between men and women, liquidity is more required for women even to guard their valued shyness and to take care of the children. I love to see a woman shy more in my privacy. That may be due to my self-interest. But, in the market, we can't afford our shyness. To make history, delete shyness at least in the market.

Are men shy? It is a subject of dispute. They jump in water even not wearing an under. Shameless guys! They are shameless only in water. When out of water, they are often more shy than their loving eves. If they are not under shyness why in a good number of houses, women are forced to emerge as family heads, breaking all conventional laws? When their own male flocks are shy, females are compelled to shell out their inherent shyness to up-bring her offspring.

The opportunity to perform like a male or a female is time bound. In my view, first twelve years, we are all children and sex neutral. Our potential to perform starts, say, at 13 and joy well end at 60; the government's time, or at 70 for the smarter. Thereafter, we are once again less classified on sex. If we honour our limited time related role based on sex, we will further break our shyness. Man and woman have to be better familiar with their biological status and consciously play of the time related role. This will help us to better address our subject, history making. The re-engineering will also enable us for the desired level performance. So, please shed the shyness. We are over bearing the burden for the last few millenniums. Leave it to Gods and relax. But, make history and seek salvation during the present life itself.

Shyness to a large extent misleads us to perpetual ignorance. It limits our opportunities, to understand and appreciate our temporary duty as Man & Woman. This creates problems to build the much needed faith and in creating a friendly atmosphere at home, at work places and even at common places. Ignorant males and shy rapped females make the life around us a mess. Instead of minding their personal business, they make themselves busy minding on others and their business. The process poses a plethora of issues. Even the much advertised gender issues, gender justice, women forums, women institutions, women queue, reservation for women even in elected forums and governments arise due to our ignorance. If it is a time related temporary phenomenon, why do we make it a national and international issue segregating men and women just in productive age? The whole subject of shame I feel is just hypocrisy created on ignorance. It is made applicable more to the majority. The minority, wielding power is relatively shameless. They break their own laws for convenience and we the majority are forced to record their history like the beach walk I mentioned, earlier. Both *Parda* and bikinis co-exist in societies at the same time experimenting. An observer gets ample opportunity to study mans' peculiar behaviour on created shame at a point of time and across the time spread over history. Dwell deep into these subjects. There is large scope for lucrative business. The smart can make money and make history.

Animals don't wear *Parda* or bikini. A few of us of late, even attempt to cover their pets. It may be due to the increasing pets invasion on man's privacy and hence the induced shame on them by us. The subject of shame and shamelessness is large and dynamic. It changes every day. Careful observation can lead to innovation worth market intervention and create wealth. The young generation may like to address the subject. To me, it is also a new avenue to create wealth and make history.

We should more cleverly monitor shyness along with our aging process. A child looks beautiful even without a shred of cloth. His shyness is liked by all. Can we appreciate adolescents when they attempt to reflect their own childhood? If someone attempt, we prefer to black paint them as mentally challenged. Many grown up wrongly however, market their shyness to capture attention. When a group of friends placed a marriage proposal to their friend's daughter before his wife, as he was abroad, an usual shyness the lady showcased as if the proposal is for her and not for her daughter, who was also witnessing the show. This is an inbuilt mental disorder worth treatment. In the absence of husband, the girl's mother would have taken the responsibility to critically assess the suitability of the boy and informed her husband to enable them to reach a suitable decision. Where is the role of shyness in the subject? In another occasion, I had to request one of my close relatives, a woman in middle age to settle the weekly wages of the carpenters working at home, as I had to be in the field on pre-scheduled work under contract. The woman showed shyness and failed to help me. Years after, I probed on her hesitancy and she told that she was scared of strangers; and in most of the films she saw such initiatives resulted in harassment and more dangerous incidents. It may be true for her, and, I don't dispute. But it needs changes. Such feelings make day-to-day business, and making history much more difficult. Majority of us confront such situation due to shyness, a larger disorder wanting changes. The groups of carpenters working at home for over 2 months had loving families at their homes. Shyness leads to ignorance and block ourselves in building mutual trust and faith. It ruins us, the majority, the vast keepers of shyness. Let it be with kids. It is beautiful to watch them in their shyness. Let us not copy them when we grow up. It will reflect only our mental sickness. Self-treatment is best treatment. Realize the limitation within and secretly come out. For making history, let us be shameless. My parents didn't do it. So I will also not do it. OK. But time has changed. You can't be shy and perform. When you climb the ladder, take care of yourself least you may not slip and break your bone and help the orthopaedic to make history. Our shyness can be an investment for them. Take care of your money, your time.

For making history we need money and time. Never submit yourself for others exploitation.

5.2 *Complex*

Complex, we shall limits its use on 'I can do' – 'I can't do'. This is inherent in each one of us. I can't do is more prevalent among us, the majority having limited history or no history. Our shyness grows within us and hatches the eggs of incapability and withdrawal from initiatives. This makes us observers and non-performers, resulting in a status of no history or limited history.

Knowing our own complex is again a self-driven exercise. Law makers can't make laws and compel you to address your own complex. We are also yet to develop methods and institutions to break each one's complex. Somehow it is within us. Realize the same; and, tune up or tune down your complex based on requirements. To emerge as performers, we have to adopt such school of thoughts. By attaining formal education, we can't break our complex. Often, it adds to the existing complex, the inferiority complex. From primary level schooling, environment at home and neighbourhood, the elements of complex start building within us. Our schooling and teachers unknowingly nurse this process, especially among the majority having no history.

Often, the stamping is done during childhood highlighting a few winners within a class room. Look he will do and you guys can't. Teachers ceremoniously make collective attempt to develop inferiority complex among their own loving students. Exemptions are always there. I'm placing the subject before you to take care of your wards. An unfortunate system of stamping the majority as weak and inculcating an inferiority complex among them is addressed currently by our teaching community. They pose themselves as Gurus and even dare to curse the students to nurse inferiority complex. In most of the educational and training programs, such process is imbibed and even unknowingly institutionalized. Often, a proud display of the merit list and topers drive away the majority from the ring with large blocks of inferiority loaded on their heads. Our educational institutions are not meant for rearing studs for developing semen banks for artificial insemination, like under dairy development. Manpower planners may like to address such issues with their new vision and action. History makers should never wait for such changes. You address the subject yourself. Never miss the time on our mission, our future history.

Presently, the process keeps away a large majority from the main stream of performance. They are not handheld to look into their own strength and to perform with efficiency. It remains less noticed and stumped out as if it is not envisaged in their curriculum and therefore not to be inclusive. Detailed studies on school dropouts and their contribution to the local economy and micro level production process are yet to be attempted. Majority of them are lost in history with their clever teacher's grades and cocky nick names. These are the traces of bitter history they leave behind. Such institutions survive among our neighbourhood inducing inferiority complex right from childhood. These institutions should trace out their meritorious students and their present locations. If you can locate a few in the local area it is worth appreciating. Or else, change yourself. Develop a strategy to handhold even the less smart who are destined to be at the local area. If incapable, exhibit a board on your teachers merit or demerit adjoining the current display boards.

If you are one among the majority and without history, you should never depend on the educational institutions proudly exhibiting students merits on display boards. If your ward is not in list his probability to make history is nipped out at the very budding stage. This is a wrong practice. The powerful minority will never like to change the system for their obvious interest in elimination to retain power. Realize the trap and learn to save yourself and your child if you want to be history makers

Of late, I was destined to observe an *Anganwady*, a baby care centre, in a village located twenty kilometre from capital city, Thiruvananthapuram. An elderly lady, unable to stand on her feet was sitting and using an unusually long stick for bobbing on the heads of babies to mind. Her duty was to keep them like a heard of sheep within the dinky porch till her daughter returns after attending her supplementary job to run the family. Govt. paid only a paltry sum to her honorary service for moulding the future generation in the largest democracy. This is the place where inferiority complex is nursed by the powerful to ensure the supply chain of targeted orderly. Elected representatives who grow up in such social structure are familiar with the subject and they don't get time to address such silly subjects. They are more on to expose corruption of their counter parts and to self-defend for survival. They live with the inherited inferiority complex and are comfortable. For my subject, future history, the players should emanate from such cells. If you are really committed to make history, address this subject. There is enough scope for future history of yours.

If you want to know the extent of inferiority complex within you, write down incidences in your memory right from childhood and your journey through time. An awareness on the subject will enable you to ward of your offspring/ sibling from its blind repetition. That appears to be the only change process you can immediately address yourself and participate in empowerment process of your kith and kin and handhold them to make their history. If this write up stimulates you, even for a second to have a thinking process triggering in you, the mission is addressed.

To hide the inferiority complex often we pretend superiority complex and project as if born great. Made up food habits, dress, body language, public relations, busy schedules, lavish spending even by borrowing, claiming proud parentage and their adventures and even thriller ghost stories are carefully casted to cover the complex. Even the media make business, showcasing our superiority complex and concealing the much owned inferiority complex. It is a business, fast developing and diversifying. A sweep on your social media will delight you seeing the crowd, its rush and its new entrants. Our minority, the powerful are experts to create myth and fantasy. And, they could successfully deploy those instruments to trap us for more than 1000 years. Now, time has changed. Never give scope for repeating the past history. Earlier, history could be made through feuds, battles, wars and world wars. Now, it is market and be with the market and with its changes shedding the inbuilt complex and face the current reality.

I request you to make further probe on the subject at your end. It is a potential area to sell like music, real estate and other services. Mans' instinct to react against on torture and their hidden ambitions to react remain unfulfilled. It is a large canvas worth marketing. Hollywood, Bollywood etc. are success models under future films. Carefully chose innovative products and services and you can attempt to fill the market and make quick bucks. Be in the market and make history. 'Don't run away'. Remember the fact that you have missed a carrying vehicle for more than 1000 years and you are left with no history. Market is the only available and the latest vehicle. Jump in to it and make history. It is right in your place. Shed the complex and realize the reality. You have nothing to lose; even not past history. The bloody complex is implanted in us. Like the Hollywood heroes remove the electronic chip from their body; we too should plug it out. The virus is there for the last one Millennium. You and I are wrongly tamed or domesticated using the chip, the COMPLEX carefully implanted. Like the cats and dogs coming out of water and jerk out water molecules, we too have to jerk it out. Make it a practice and institutionalize. Or, count days for severe peril. If any get extraordinary eye brow twist, watch out, he/she can be the one with the hidden noose; like the long stick with a dog trap.

5.3 *Culture*

I am not on Vedic, Indo-Aryan, Egyptian, European, or Mayans' culture. I'm on the subject the culture of you and I and our culture at home; the culture of the majority, the target group with no history or less history. Do we have a culture of our own? If so, what is it? Are we really proud of our culture, or, posing to possess something like invisible? Are we capable to frame and internalize a culture of our liking, for ourselves and at our homes? These statements are worth hearing and for imagination. But can we write down a few points on our 'proud culture'? If so, write it on a note book or your computer or on you smart phone, the culture within you and you observe at your home. Please attempt.

If you feel proud of your culture and adhere to the same at home, hats off. You are a winner. If you are confused, it is worth for a relook on the subject by yourself. The subject is opened and you are the only person on earth who can address the subject; and if necessary, change your traits, your culture for the period leftover to you. Culture has something relating to your daily practice. Hence, it is your subject. Others cannot practice on behalf of you. For the time being, forget the culture we excavated at Harappa and Mohenjo-Daro. Be with the present; and work on the subject. It's rewarding.

While addressing the above subject, we have to be aware of our limitation. Our existing culture has fixed a scale or a unit for our performance, like a measuring glass. How much you have filled in and what is the leftover space available to, you should know yourself. The measuring glass may be elastic one, for you. To some others, it may be non-elastic, say like metallic. In both the type you can fill. If necessary, replace the old stuff with the newly found, the new culture, you value. You can enjoy your life and make history. If you have elastic one, you are perhaps, the one blessed and born privileged. You can fill in, what you want; what you are in love with. But choose your items to fill. The stuff selected should be life term worth enjoyable and also leave something worth to your immediate kith and kin making your history, and you should also enjoy while making, recording and recollecting your history. We are on history making. A better culture will enable us to make proud history and leave for the next generation. Unfortunately, we have at home a culture requiring refinement to showcase. Climb your stairs and showcase. Never preach on culture. But practice. You will make history.

Those with metallic one, do have a careful look. Perhaps, it may be elastic and due to accumulated dust, dirt and rust it might have lost its elasticity. Rub on them, and if you are successful, you too emerge as history makers, shunting the old and filling the new and making innovation in the market and empowering your kith not to waste time on venture capital, mostly booked for those having history and you are misled to read on ad-paper. Use your energy to discover yourself; your elasticity will increase your own capability to perform. Don't waste time in malls and surfing. Surf yourself and find yourself to optimize your own capacity. Take care that you are not stamped out due to the nearing expiry date without making history. Just initiate the process and get yourself enlisted in history making. All metallic can be made elastic, if you work on it.

Monuments which are on the surface of the planet are owned by the powerful, the minority. Where is your space, by which you can be proud of? I couldn't't so far observe my forefathers in them. Perhaps, our history lies beneath the earth yet to be excavated. Time has hidden them and we are all having short history or no history like lord Buddha in Indian sub-continent where he once preached. The minority wielding power has hidden our history, the majority of the common mans' history. Truth is beneath our feet. It is time to unearth and find ourselves. Don't leave the subject to the present historians. Their specialization is on serving the rich and the powerful and earn for their sustenance. The clever make *ladoos,* a savoury, for business. Our mythology is such *ladoos* made by those clever receiving payment. The subject taught to us as history is paid history. For making such history, they had destroyed us and even traces of our culture. If we are still proud of our culture, know thy self and embrace thy's. Note the cooked up history and the blind practices of them had emerged as a culture, mostly of mutual hatred. I was moulded to dream Gods with AK 47. And, it took a long time for me to replace them with models of teachers. It happens after retirement, after 60 years of bondage. During my college days the economy was made to crawl by a few history makers marketing mythology through wires. It slowed down the growth process. During that time, the entire sub-continent was halted for more than an hour when a mythical story was telecasted. The proud culture resulted in stagnant growth and an economist termed it as 'Hindu Rate of Growth'; i.e. <3%. A school student was compelled to ask the President of the largest democracy in the world, 'Sir, can I ever live in a developed country? The scientist turned first citizen smiled and happily passed away leaving the question to the majority without history. Reaching the Mars is easy, but changing the mind-set of us is not easy; because, in a democracy, you only can fire your rocket. When others fire at you, it becomes a crime. So, internalize a new culture to ignite yourself to a desired culture. Make yourself more elastic to be in the market.

Through careful care, the clever will try to sell their old wines in new bottles. There are smart methods of marketing even the rotten fish. Be careful to get carried off amidst wrong advertisements. Your, near and dear may hold tight their metallic measuring units may hesitate to enthral anything new you prefer to internalize. They are like cancerous cells; but definitely curative. Once got in, they will suck you near to death and celebrate. It is our inbuilt culture. It happens due to our collective ignorance. But, they are an army of themselves. Like your aptitude on moulding a new culture, they have a much stronger attitude against the market friendly culture. Attitudinal shift is though not impossible, but difficult within your short life span left. The great circus will continue. Learn to jump like Kangaroo. Switchover to the fast changing market culture and learn to live in the new bus without missing your bus. The so called proud culture can be your Villain. Never allow HIM to hold you; and, prevent you to badge in. The next bus may reach you after 1000 years as happened in our proud history. Our forefathers were captive during those golden days to make history of Gods and God man, the privileged and self-declared. They could definitely make their history and well enjoy their life. If you are a student of history, think what happened to your forefathers during such golden period? That will stimulate and recharge your genes on the subject.

Prospective history makers perhaps would love to build partnership with those having elastic measuring vessels. Through careful observations, you can choose your partner, your friend, your spouse, your business partner, your colleagues and market operators familiar to you. If you are in two boats, two culture, it is next to impossible for partnership building other than biological, social needs and reproduction. Those are possible and therefore, less market related. Prices are affixed on marketed produce, products and service. I'm sharing a few thinking process on market led operations; and, not on the familiar mutual service for which partnership can be temporarily built for mutual care, pleasure, convenience and satisfaction.

A culture helpful for history building process is yet to be attained by majority of our family. Presently, we are sheltered mostly under a practice for substance living and for biological reasons. Partnership building for market operations is different and they are to be internalized.

The much often heard from queen's mouth at home is that "don't talk business at home. Leave them there at your work place and be with me and for us". It is our primitive culture and further strengthened by cinematic dialogue. A youth in a developing country's backdrop has no place where he can share his views on wealth creation. At home, we don't allow him to open up. But petty talks on latest film or serials and their hero and even their personal life become hot subjects for endless deliberations. Earlier it was mythology and now through the new media, new *avathars*, incarnations are innovated and showcased. It is our culture to look across the fence or walls. During our community life earlier, perhaps, this curiosity might have emerged in our genes for our own self defence, sustainability and for entertainment. Now our living style has changed. We have to have new and market friendly methods to live and learn to live making use of the market. A new culture has to be nursed to keep ourselves in the track and be in the new bus; the market and its vide spectrum, under the caption, globalization. It's the new religion. Babtise and be in the new bus. After some time, another bus may emerge. Getting into the latest bus will be better possible for your children or your grandchildren, if you are in the current running bus. We have no history on those who missed the earlier buses. Historians, call them aboriginal. Do you want to see your great grandchildren under a similar tagged group? You decide.

For us the majority, there is no other space other than our family. There is also none other than the family members to build partnership. In the market, both men and materials are priced. We don't have money to build a corporate office and invite resource persons and brain storm on our innovative ideas. It can be first shared within the family only.

But the metallic culture at home drives the innovator out. Even a patient hearing is painful to us. The same group will preach before the idiot box and weep on the familiar drama, jerking tears. It is the static or metallic culture. The present culture is carefully designed to ensure labour supply under sustenance wage. To ensure the same, our entertainment programs are carefully designed. Unfortunately, our women are used for this re-engineering. They are tuned to be their agents. They are misled to operate for the powerful and not for the family. It happened more among the families with no history. Realize the self-built fabrics on bonding and their continuation. Plug them out from the nexus. You have to have the determination to make your own history. There is an urgent need for a thorough revamp on our culture to make our own history.

A careful look on your family will reveal the plot as it is in a TV serial. You initiate anything at home; they will collectively first find your place out of their mind; and, subsequently even from your shelter. We have to salute those champions who could introduce the existing culture. They were successful in implanting the genes on servility in the majority and even today, they continue to have a large market share using the enslaved. We are tuned to outcaste our own daughters on slight violation of their rules. Many of us are tuned to work as agents to translate their well-designed culture. Religious and social gatherings are used to further strengthen the system. And, you and I, the majority, are trapped for internalization of the rules of them, the powerful. The process keeps the minority to hold the power to rule you and I, the majority without history. Make changes within you and in your family, if possible. Because, when you initiate a change, there can be great wars at home. But, learn to smile and bring in the change. Be a change agent at home. Internalize your own well-chosen culture for market related growth. Forget the past. If required, unlearn. The slave in us and at home are to be killed through cultural change. That will ensure our future history in the market economy. Once you have money, you can bring in at your home, all saleable.

Our present culture at home looks down to the family head returning after a day's toil outside. His dress, sweat and tired face are not a match with those they witnessed on T.V. by using the remote and pressing their fingers. With slight efforts, their metallic containers were filled with the stuff they were aspiring, perhaps through ages. The tired man find the wine shops' bench more accommodating and friends there listening to his days' stories and innovation. The history maker is displaced. The metallic culture limits their scope to develop resentment at home and left only with obesity to showcase. Those having a different way of thinking is thrown out of their shelter, mentally, physically and often to the deep woods forcing them to search for their old culture and lost Gurus with the dried up genes. Open your third eye and you can observe this mystic culture at home. If you're different, I'm happy.

Attached to the word culture, the often quoted word is revolution, Cultural Revolution. I fail to observe fruits of any revolution around me. It may be my limitation. You have a self-search and if possible, attempt a search on your family members too? If you can find fruits through any recent revolution, I am happy. Unfortunately, I could so far more frequently observe elements of degradation only. Blind followers of the earlier culture had degraded their overall culture of their family. May be a very peculiar happening, I observe in my neighbourhood. We make our family members shy, non-performers and keep them away from markets and its competition. The process weaken us the majority, strengthening only the supply chains of labour even to far of places. Among the youth, the capable we pick up and we shunt them out to earn; and the weak, is accommodated at home and they further degrade the local economy and its culture. A queen at home and the weak male rule the roost; and it is celebrated with the regular remittance or M.O. they receive. As the leadership also emerges from the leftover weak, it reflects on perpetual poor governance. For hiding the truth, lies are spread repeatedly and it is made truth. A new culture is unknowingly internalized.

A culture to earn through value addition remains a cultureless activity among us. That is our culture. A young entrepreneur finds difficulty in getting a matching girl for marriage under this culture. But an office attendant will be hunted out and crowned. The culture of encouraging the weak on the new zeal to ensure social security has opened up added scope for even the mediocre to make history. We should make use of them and in real spirit never forget to probe in to the avenues for making supplementary income from the market. Otherwise like the earlier invaders, captions of the new market will suck us like the lizards on your walls at home. Of late, I was forced to read history, which I still believe as cock and bull stories and adventures of our petty kings even taxing on the breast of their subjects; our loving grannies. Using a simple item, mirror, he could have located better taxable item to be taxed. It is history; recorded history in southern part of India. A lady chopped them off in protest. It remains yet to be recorded in the government manual. In sponsored history she is yet to find a place. It also await for attention of the historians and even film makers. They think that it is a shameful item of their own history and therefore, not fit for coverage. Unfortunately, it is our own history; but we feel shame on our 'proud' culture.

Our women, even the women born and brought up by the powerful are not in history. If the culture is of any value, why they had thrown out their own daughters when they made attempts to step out from the culture they disliked? Rather, they were tagged, pushed out of home and even secretly traded. That is true history. It was a business even during the recent past. All such nasty things we had done to keep up an imported culture; a God made culture, air dropped, direct from the heavens. Existence of such a culture and their practice was real and not mythical. A black magic marketing concept like Maya, illusion was used to enslave the majority and the weak especially the women, by microscopic minority claiming descendants of the culture. The youth should probe on the subject and drag out the true skeleton; the true culture. It's there in our cupboards in each home. Those skeletons once pulled out will empower you to make your home a better sweet home and you will develop a culture of yourself to be in history. It's value addition at home. Women at homes are the best to address such change process. Your kids will bring back larger returns on your efforts on value addition at home. This will concretize your role in future history.

Cultural changes are possible at home mostly through women. Therefore, such changes at home may take time. Women are busy and they don't find time for change. Earlier, taking care of the average half-a-dozen children in a joint family and the agriculture activity was drudgery. During the past, there was less time and freedom to accept anything new and unlisted. Over time, considerable changes had come in the management of home. In place of earlier joint family, currently it is nuclear family, with one or two children. Our homes are also equipped with new home appliance, phone and computer connectivity and vehicle for movements. The time we gained is currently stolen by the T.V. at home. Most of its programs sell our lost proud culture and related family issues. There is ample scope for the young, especially women entrepreneurs, to innovate and make money using the time gained by a large segment of our women.

Cultural changes are possible through media, provided the producers have innovative culture in their genes. To sell a light drink we may not scratch on culture and it a truth. But if we fail to make use of the time gained, unlike earlier farting of the fakirs it will create more tremors in our drawing room by the obese with catalyst like aerated drinks and junk food. Such symptoms are bad reflections on our happy life. That makes them aliens at home. With a duel culture at home, your work on history making will be difficult. This is a limiting factor to make history at home by the majority. Realize the same, change and emerge as history makers handholding even those entering in Limca Book on obesity. Our women can play increasing role on the subject. The petty Rajas, if alive would have located another revenue resource of the obese, worth taxing. Their cunning *Devans,* ministers would have put up a note that obese have eaten the food of others, and therefore, it is worth taxing them based on their body weight. Anyone above 75 kg may be taxed; irrespective of sex; minority, the powerful as usual may be exempted. We, the history makers are to be trim so that we can jump, dance and enjoy life; leaving history at least for our loving children. Women liberation volunteers and change agents may encourage women entrepreneurs to excel in the market and address women empowerment. That will create new history leading to a bright future history.

What history a non-performer and self-arrested at home can make? A few of my own relatives are counting days in their flats in cities. They were educated and finding a job, 40 years back in a metro would have empowered them to be trim and draw a decent pension and fly to nearby countries for holidays. Their much loved culture trapped them at home. During elderly age, many of them are unable to climb down from those old flats having no lift. They are almost under house arrest. The T.V. programs keep them alive. Attachment with our earlier culture was too good in making us and our woman, non-performers. Traces of slavery still dominate in our DNA. Don't curse others. Curse ourselves for the culture we adore. Don't celebrate failure. It is bad a culture. In my generation, many of us missed even the slow moving bus. We were at a transitional stage. Those who missed the bus, added to the large army, without history. That is our history. Take care of yourself and don't follow us. Never make the mistake of waiting for any. You board on your moving bus and ensure your history. Nature will take care of us, the elderly; in her cycling process. And, we will get recycled and get *Moksha*, reserved for us. Sorry, we fail to make our history. We were misled by a missing culture. Search, you'll realize.

Episode 6

Leader, Labour and Sucker

6.1 Leader

We, the majority, having no history or less history are a set of dreamers. Most of us love to be kings like earlier Pharos, Alexander, Napoleon, Emperor Asoka or Akbar the Great. We love to be kings and queens. In my childhood, I used to ride on a white horse with flowing rob and tightly fixed crown with angels as pillion riders. Our earlier kings were successful to insert their charms in our DNA. And, we love wielding power and exhibiting kingly traits. But, rarely we like to be hand holders like Lord Buddha, Jesus Christ, Prophet Nabi or Guru Nanak. They too were leaders and are still powerful even after their death. But, I never dreamt to be one of them. At this elderly age, I wonder why? Even today, I don't want to be one among them, not even Mahatma Gandhi! Perhaps, they are yet to get into my genes, our genes, the genes of majority. It may be a discomforting truth.

Of late, there is no scope to be kings and queens. Perhaps, that is why many of us behave like kings and queens at home. Often, our own queen over throw us and capture power in her kingdom, within the four walls of her citadel. A cope at home and lady assuming power is silently tolerated by the cultured at home. Clever among us coronate the queen and claim selfless, OK you be queen at home and I'm king outside, as the Sardar under Sikh faith jokes. Between the two sex, male make claims for more power and females wield them. Thus, the life of music moves synchronizing with the familiar Sound of Music; in the classic film. Value based surrender for co-existence. Now, you probe into the leader at your home.

The kings in history had evidence for a short period. But in wild life, the power-wielding process has bonding with nature. We too might have learnt the tricks from nature. Anyway, it is with us. And I think, it is more with the majority, yet to acquire power. Therefore, they have less history or no history and no money like most of us. If you buy my book I'm in history. The attempt is made, and your purse is my target. I'm trying to be in the market to be in history. Don't hesitate to join. Don't miss the bus. Consciously read the book; and, internalize your favourite bites. That will help you to have a search of the leader in you and make your history.

In this episode, we will look into the great circus going around leaders, workers and a large cross section of the suckers, the clever. Between the leader and sucker, the worker constituting the sizable is milked even in their dry stage. The workers are used and thrown. Of late, waste bins are institutionalized to contain them. They are nowhere in history. To a large extent, we are responsible for the same. The great changes envisaged in favour of the workers are currently drawing less attention in the market led global changes. Leadership therefore need new evolution to make history. It's an opportunity to the majority wanting to be in history.

We have an inborn or inherited DNA to produce our own leaders. To me, it appears a wild behaviour, more befitting to the jungle, even in the upcoming concrete jungle in your neighbourhood. To work under wilderness, we need a leader, may be to tame ourselves. We are less human; and, more still of animals' traits. We can't behave ourselves and we need policing. So, we produce leaders to rule us. Leaders in return, make us scrawl, roll and even to dance before them. The cosmic dance goes on. We somehow love it. It has long, very long history. That is the true history of ours and worth laughing. But time has changed. Stop the pre-scripted cosmic dance. Please listen to the tune of the market. Learn to dance in the emerging market making money and history. That is a challenge and we have to confront the reality to be in history.

In the present scenario, the cosmic dance we have at home. We empower one among ourselves and coronate.

When he starts using his power, we restrain ourselves. We start cursing the powerful. They become alienated wielding power; controlling all productive resources, including you. Laws on imposing power and controlling resource result. This leads to first feuds, then fight, breakage or surrender and slavery. Love, compassion and care fade away. It remains in the memory of a few as theories. The history part of them, we already burnt. When we had a relatively better leader, we had better productive efficiency, sizable leisure and we enjoyed singing, dancing, searching our roots and smiling like the enlightened. But, we buried those cultures due to wrong leadership. In the new order, Love, Peace, Care and Happiness, the old stuff was promised after death. That was our recent history. Perhaps, Life Insurance might have made use of that culture to make their business. That is their history. First die, and then, enjoy seeing your own people use or misuse your money.

In both the process, we need leaders. Without leadership we lack the skill to live our life, because we are wild. We have to be tamed and controlled. We are more familiar with the wild cats and their leaders and their territory. Thus, we have to abide the wild laws. Humanitarianism is more academic. It remains in the minds of a few and in unread books and not saleable products. So our T.V. programs are loaded with those serials telling stories on our wild nature at home. Stories of the normal human beings are not worth for selling. They are on nascent stage and time will perhaps make them saleable.

Now, let us concentrate on saleable. Let us be in the market and be wild and aggressive in the market with killer instinct. Awaken the leader in you. Empower him to be aggressive in the market and showcase him as the leader. The leader is always made. You can make yourself the leader in your market. Under liberalized current scenario, it is possible when you shed your shyness and allow the king in you to be the market leader. That is history making. You trigger yourself and the king in you can be reshaped to be the leader in the market. With money, the market will provide you all kingly settings you longed for in your dreams. Translating dreams to reality is history making.

Of late, in place of old kings, similar to the clan of their advisers, clergy, sycophants and even eunuch have assumed power. They train their youth preferably having no history to pelt stones on both private and government properties, introducing strikes, harthals, bandhs, creating atrocities and specializing on destruction which are easy because they daily practice at home and in their neighbourhood. Through acquired power, they carry on corruption, their institutionalization, building partnership with cross section of the public, police, judiciary, smugglers, terrorist, and insurgents from neighbourhood, defence forces, secret services, self-posing saviours and even patriots on earth. A competition on building partnership to acquire power is highlighted and appreciated by media and paid writers as political skill. Political leaders booked and punished by judiciary, with corruption, re-emerge as champions with varied experience. Earlier gap of shameful with the shameless is filled in, making scope for new types of collations and history. The market on corruption is well opened up. It's your choice whether you like to take part and make history. It is a reality and opportunity.

Under the emerging decentralization of power, locally elected peoples' representatives also emerge from the leftover, the majority, with no history. It is a welcome feature. However, they are controlled by their leaders, the powerful from above. Together they practice corruption and resulting in empowerment of the same minority. But, they preach socialism and the means, they are not bothered. Sharing power to practice corruption and building its own new hierarchy wherein the shameless only have larger scope for making history. A larger opportunity can also be traced if you can forget the leader from above, and take the local leadership, wield power and make history. It's a change process and what you need is not money, but guts. Acquire the same, capture power in Local Self Governance like Panchayat, perform and change your history. You will be in history. The avenue is right before you. Through timely fit leadership, you can make history. If you have knowledge and skill, it will open up new avenues for marketing new history of the local area; which is missing for a few centuries.

The process will initiate the production of leaders and ensure regular supply chain under the market of politics to grab power. For survival, we have to be performers in the new market. Or else, we will be thrown out of market; and our 'party' will get extinct. Others will get extinct in history of politics. Quoting the history of earlier political leaders, the new set often highlights the extinction of the non-corrupt from even history. Only the corrupt could survive in our recent politics. The new set is helpless other than follow the beaten track. This creates large scope for new platforms. If you're different, address the subject and make future history.

The leadership at home and in the neighbourhood is undergoing great changes, making history. It is time for the majority to participate. Forget the earlier history of folding hands, thinking on virtues and shyness on participation. We have done the same, enough and more during the last 4000 years. Jump in the foray and participate. In the process you will not miss the time and pushed behind, without history. Make innovation on the system. Get empowered and make history. All the suckers, have made history and we are forced to read them. I'm not jealous. But they used us, the majority to suck and climbed on us wielding power. It is worth realizing. It helps at least in recovery from the current degraded and stamped status. Wealth can be created through efficiency and even miss use of power. The first one is time taking. So make use of the second, it is well available at your door step. Make use of the opportunity. The leadership in you will emerge. Leaders don't advocate this method. But they do practice to be in history. We're yet to find a LEADER, accepting the fact that he is/was corrupt. So can we draw an inference that to be a leader, one has to be a lier? If majority of us start practicing the fact, what will be the future history? So, learn to shunt the leader and make history by assuming right kind of leadership. That will ensure you to be in future history. It's an art presently unknown. It can emerge only from the leftover, without history. You trigger the leader in you. The process will ensure the history of yours, the majority, the leftover.

The king, queen and the leader is hidden in you. Trigger the DNA, realize and perform. For winning, choose your own method. That will bring in variety in market operations, their specialization and building your leadership quality. When you climb up the ladder, you will not be forced to carry the cross, we kept on the weak shoulders of Jesus for doing good things. It is history. Let us not worry ourselves, who are yet to make history. We have nothing left, not even shame. Tears are our only assets. Preserve them. Let us shed it after retirement, say after 65, reading scriptures and awaiting the punishments for our sins in corporate hospitals in the company of our living Mantrijis; the ministers, the leaders. Internalize the new art of creating new leadership. Innovate. Only you can do it. The minority has limitation. Corruption has become cancerous and viral among them. It's in their gene and they have to live with it.

Can we together practice corruption and say, it is for survival? The present schools on leadership are forced to practice corruption to retain their leadership. The youth familiar with alternate market opportunity can always think differently. To make history, quick money is required and there is no alternative. In political market, now perfect market competition is in operation, at least in corruption. Let us compete and those successful will survive. As none of the political parties generate income, this happens to be the only source of survival. Join the process. It will ensure perfect competition. In between two general elections there is 5 year long period. How can anyone survive in a market driven economy without money? All established political parties understood the subject. Only the public, especially those without history, fail to realize the fact and they swing along with the wind, storm, or latest tornado. Stop swinging. Hold the rope, develop skill, emerge as leaders and make future history. If you don't like the words corruption and leadership invent new words for satisfaction. But, never miss the platform. Earlier the powerful used the words like ghost and hounded house to ward off us, the majority. Subsequently, touchability and untouchability and even trade marks were used to keep us away from the main stream. Learn the tricks from our loving leaders and make history following their footsteps. They will be less happy. But they are helpless in preventing you from market operations. Make use of the opportunity. That will ensure avenues for new history and innovations on leadership.

6.2 Labor

Communist Manifesto focused on labour. Majority with scarce history are stamped under this category. Whether we are on sea port, airport, railways, banks, civil administration, farm and non-farm based, any profession like law medicine, engineering, I.T. communication, you and I are mostly labour; those render their services for wages, perks and of late, a microscopic minority sharing even profit. It is the working class paid; and often not paid, like the housewife or a volunteer worker, the unknown toiling throughout the world. In limited sense, labour is that segment which can be hired and fired under market mechanism. Stalwarts like Karl Marx attempted to trace their history and made efforts to empower them, obviously with their short history. Most of them, dominate the world with no traceable history of them. In the newly emerging market, like the earlier privileged class and caste system, the new tribe wears tailored uniforms. Most of them are also proud off their dress codes. During the time of touchable and untouchable, slaves, contract or bonded labour, most of them were without dress, wearing *Lankoty*, nick-named Indian-tie. They became a part of the history with no history. Under the new market in place of earlier barbers, tailors and others a set of new breed of them make history by stitching uniforms, and marketing better health care and face lift. Right from priest class, the direct servants of the God class, down to rag-picker, exempting a few like pick-pockets, all are in tailored uniforms. Through a variety of uniforms, the mighty working class, the actual the human efforts behind the agri-produces, industrial products and the mighty service providers are better showcased in the current market focusing on profit to make history, by the market leaders, the emerging powerful.

Majority of the target group are scattered, and contribute their labour, get tired and go to deep sleep to wake up and attend next day chorus. Though they are the majority, they remain cut off from the daily happenings at home, on streets and market. The morning ad: papers and the streaks of news available in between the advertisements are the limited news and knowledge they generally have from their surroundings. They are further facilitated by their managers or the skilled workers, on their job to enable them to work more to maximize profit.

The large segment, right from defence service to the village level service providers are the labour, both under private and public sector and at home engaged to execute the work. The much talked 8 hours work is on paper. Most of them are on 12 hours duty. In cities they travel on an average 4 hours in a day to attend their duty and to return home. When tired, they sleep anywhere to recharge themselves. They don't have time to make history. They make goods and commodities and provide all services and enable others, especially with power, to make history. History writers generally avoid them, may be due to their own poverty and helplessness. They are forced to write in favour of those who pay them. I too was in the process for 32 years. Any deviation from convention my boss corrected; with gestures 'Look back and go ahead'. As there was no history on majority, our team recorded only for the powerful those who placed our boss, including governments. That was our collective historical contribution. Now I realize that this large segment with no history is always taken into granted.

The very survival of this vast majority is yet to get acknowledged even at home, in the neighbourhood, in their own work places and in the market. They are found less in history in our cables, in our ad-papers and not even in our gossip. When we charge our cell phones, we do not think on electricity or the flow of electron. When we eat an apple only the mad think about the orchard, the farmer, the farm labour or the one who transported and made it available to the market. They are the labour; and why should we mind them? We are concerned on the apple, its price and its taste. Like the dupes in commercial films, all work to project the hero and he becomes the subject of the mentally challenged. The dupes are not in our memory. They are Maya. The actor flexes his muscle and hips. We have business only with those items we buy or see or hear. The apple and the heroes get into our mind and in our history. On the process, we forget the labour and the real hero and we continue to ensure our status, not in history. It's stupidity. Let us be aware of our own role in self-elimination from history.

I make an attempt to expose the value of labour in you and I and encourage you to make a self-search. I know, many of you may not have time for the same. If you can't have the time, make yourself aware of the subject and your kids will address. That is life, and there is scope for making our history. It is worth trying. It is empowerment, money making, wealth creating and will enable us to make future history. Forget the past; 'All workers of the world unite'. We failed to unite and became redundant. Think on alternate slogans. Perhaps, your wards will make them. They will write your history, a future history, a new empowerment process. Just allow them. Never tell the mythical stories to them. Let them be free and allow them to learn from the market. Like the T.V. programs, mythical stories were used for marketing selected products and services and to trap the majority. They were highly successful. That is why even today they could sell them to us. The minority, the powerful, like my boss, never sit before T.V. and waste time. If you are on history making, you need time. Find time to awake the leader in you. History will follow.

You might have seen a few statues on side of roads. Do you have one of the local labour there? A farmer, a weaver, a skilled or unskilled worker or a house wife etc. are yet to be seen on those statues. They are destined to play 'statue' only during childhood. I am yet to see them in statues. In Lenin square it is there to market their leaders, and not the real labour. An expired labour, you may find in ad papers under obituary, if his/her wards are money powered. In metros, it is on extinct due to un-affordability. I could more frequently trace their obituary note only on photo frames on the walls of their houses. I have found a few statues of the leaders, perhaps those with power to make their own statue, when alive. As birds are ignorant of their power, they continue to dirt on them. If their wards are in power, they use our money and ask one of us, the labour, to wash and clean. It is our duty. It was our ancestral duty. Much water has flown, but history remains, unchanged. You did your duties sincerely not even realizing the power of power & money and the role you played in history making for them. The labour, is not having time. They are at work. Their faculty on work only has developed. It remained numb on the need to make their role in history. The touchable & untouchable, slaves & masters, the marginalized & the down trodden are currently dead and vanished from national statistics. Most of them got terminated with no history. The process goes on, rubbing out the poor with the scrubber. No traces of them even today. For keeping power and making money, the powerful are of late, more in the market. Learn from them. Get into the market and be a market leader if you are on your future history.

The present labour has emerged observing earlier leaders and even suckers. We have a new style, the hero tosses a coin to catch attention like the umpire in cricket to choose the team for batting. Drawing attention is an art. Films and cricket could prove them. They are empowered with name and fame. Art of maintaining the celebrity status itself is an avenue for new business. Much we can learn from them to make an entry, capture leadership in the market, and make money and to make history. It is required for the very survival. By initiating, you can realize your capacity and your true history, and the great efforts of the powerful to drive you to the walls. To me, a shift from labour to entrepreneur only will enable us to make history, in the present market. I may be biased, based on my background in the subject, economics. But, I don't find any alternative. Focus on enterprise development. Even the earlier switch over from less performing Chaityas of the weakening Buddhism, to the modern temples, appears to be a great shift to establish new enterprises for income generation. Even introduction of the Service Sector might have happened during such periods; may be a 1000 year back, which is before 30 generations. Let us learn from our own past. Let us march to the market and rejuvenate our genes to be inclusive in globalization as envisaged under our national/international agenda.

Market is the new bus. Step into the bus and establish an enterprise, even micro-enterprise is enough to begin with. Never leave your present job. Find time and trace out the entrepreneur in you. Give him space to perform. Learn from your boss and leaders how to do things behind the camera. In market operations, it is not corruption or sin. It's conversion to the new order; like the earlier change happened in our faith. Let us help our elected leaders to realize their dreams. Let us also not make aware of our leaders on the great mistake they are doing by making us inclusive and losing their own 1000 year old power gained through shedding blood and marketing mythology manufactured by the captive intellectual like our current I.T. professionals burning mid-night oil to create wealth through an alternate strategy. History repeats. The reach was earlier through myth. Now it is through computers and smart phones. We are all trapped in the market. Beware, and make use of the changing market and switch over from labour to market operators and leaders. That will ensure your history, your future history. Please attempt.

A shift from labour is often heard as next to impossible. I have grown up hearing statements like shift of a farm labour will take centuries to become a farmer. It may be true, perhaps earlier, when illiteracy was common and the market operations limited and restricted. Now, switchover is relatively better easy. We can learn the alphabets on the great switchover at least standing and watching at the periphery of established market. Focusing on your skill, trade or service, a conversion or shift to establish an enterprise is worth attempting to make history. Realize the fact that entrepreneurs are made by self. It is not otherwise. Your energy, focusing, initiatives and patience are a must for enterprise development and enabling to attempt the great leap from labour. Remember you are alone in the process. Support services may not be available to you. Never depend even your own people. They will ensure your failure. If you are successful, they may even doubt on the purity of your blood. It's due to an inherent disorder with us. Realize. If you continue to strike success all will be around you. That is the magic, the great circus to your future history. There will emerge many claimants behind successful entrepreneurs. Use them for advertisement.

Of late, quite often we hear success stories of new entrepreneurs and the innovations they are at. The advantage in you as a labour is that you have a backing on the subject for centuries. You know the pain, pressure and skill behind the building process. It is also a vital factor of production and you should rely on them. Earlier, the stress was on land, labour, capital and management. Presently, it is more relating to your zeal, the will and efficiency in using all the above items. Others will follow. Efficiency, economies of scale, market acceptance etc. are obviously vital; and like coke and pizza you can buy from market. A mind-set to break the old stamp and to rejuvenate the gene in you is of importance. Your own near and dear will be the first to scare you. They will not co-operate. They are aware of the success stories of Micro Soft or Infosys, their team building and their female's role. It is a subject worth admiring, but not to be adapted and supported at home. They are tied down as guardians of their earlier 'rich' tradition. They can maximum pray for you, perhaps even siphoning your venture capital to Gods. It is nothing but mental slavery, and they are unfortunately trapped in it. But you can break your shell. Be an entrepreneur. Be a leader. Make your history. Your success stories will emerge as role models within your family and neighbourhood. The very concept on present leadership, you can change through your mighty switchover. Future leaders will be those who win in the switch over process. If you are helpless, you may enable your own kids to jump. True leader is the one who can trace all factors of production around him and efficiently use them to produce surplus, the wealth, the new history – future history.

6.3 Sucker

I love them. Most of them are at home. You don't waste time on searching them. Your smile itself may be an unknown reflection on realizing the sucker in you. It is within our gene. Given an opportunity each one of us will perform; leaning on others when capable to stand on once own foot. Suckers are not bad. They are not trespassers, thieves, burglars, pickpockets, chain snatchers, looters, terrorists, rapists or the corrupt. They love to live on the sweat and blood of others like the mosquitoes and the bed-bugs. Suckers are our well-wishers. No mosquitoes will ever suck you to death. But Malaria and other disease they spread will land you in trouble. So, let us take care of them; to make ourselves alive and to make our history and achieve our mission.

Suckers are friendly. They move with a smile, well dressed, pretending love, care and compassion. But, beware of them. Those are pretensions for their survival. We allow them to lean, for want of the above; smile, care, love and compassion which are rare in the market and even among ourselves. Suckers being clever, they extend the rare services and capture your goodwill, suck and enjoy your sweat and blood.

A few of them are even successful in making their history. One can see a variety of successful suckers in mythology. They are with us, take care of them. You can even use them for making your history.

Our gene can have qualities inborn or acquired. Even among twins, one can observe different qualities right from conception. Perhaps, it is natures' will and design. But, we have to be conscious of our own genes especially those interested in history making. Realize them. Appreciate their merits and ward yourselves or you will be sucked and exploited as in the past. Suckers after wielding power, will behave like kings and queens. They will be helpless not to treat you and I above slaves to take care of themselves and continue to suck. It is in our DNA, the history inherited, which can repeat and we will again be victimized. The process goes on under the newly fashioned freedom and the much advertised liberalization and globalization. Habits seldom die. Freedom we should make use for self-protection and market intervention. That will build firm foundation to make history.

Suckers now penetrate in your house even through cable. Of late, sucking is a clever business better institutionalized. Instead of direct sucking like the mosquitoes, the corporate trained use world beauties, celebrities, actors, sport persons and even the emerging market leaders to skilfully execute the well-designed action points advocated and are market tested by their managers. Plethora of institutions use the models and the professionals to achieve their corporate goals. When you look at things on screens or market, develop patience also to look at the skill of suckers. They are at their work. Observe them; if possible, copy them, if you like. It is not a sin or crime. You have to guard yourself. It is an art and we with short history are to be more careful to avoid suckers and learn the tricks of their trade. If required, use it as a launching pad for market entry. You may need their traits to make your history. In the long run, you can well choose your trade based on your liking, aptitude and perception.

Even if you choose sucking a way of your sustenance, growth and history making, don't be shy. You go ahead. We are more interested in making history of ourselves. If the market is conducive and you have skill and confidence, establish yourself and emerge as a champion, making history. Never allow to be stumped out as happened early. Learn to play within the market and capture it for your advantage. The inherent gene, due to lack of experience and exposure may pose shyness to initiate. Break them. Carry only those sailing with you. Never allow anyone to stop your initiatives. Forget the earlier concept on sin. In the present market for survival, you invent your own tools. That is nothing, but history making.

Suckers using their own skill are experts in using others skill and knowledge and even their money purse. If you have doubts, you start looking for skill of those within your own family. You can well observe and appreciate their skill. Don't be jealous of them. That will break basic structure of your institution, your family, and you will be nowhere in history. Be innovative. If you could locate the skill within your family, make use of it in the market. Perhaps, you may have an added skill on their market based operations. In the process, together you can make history.

Many of us, the short-history clan, often cry on our resource crunch. We are rich with resources. But, we are yet to develop a skill to search and find our own strength. We worry more on our weakness and hesitate to explore ourselves and the minority exploits us. Tears are earmarked for us, the majority and especially for our woman. They have a skill to beat on their chest and wale. Corporate women, I feel, rarely wale like them. Whether, the subject is worth for further probing? You have the skill to find out. I leave the job to you. Hypothesis like urban women cry less than rural women, employed women have dry eyes, serial producers never cry and it is the privilege of the viewers and they never trespass, are worth testing. These are a few tools used by the clever in the market to make money and make their history. It is fun to realize the skill of entrepreneurs who make others cry and they do profitable business. Let us learn from them. They are masters in making our obese jerk out their tears. When we fail at home, they make grant success by making us to mourn even at national level at scheduled time. The process can shape our new genes for punctuality to morn, like our habit to brush our teeth. How you make them change, can be a subject under history, if you are successful. If they mourn on your attempt, leave them like when you are trapped in a boring movie in a shabby theatre. If time and resource are favourable, you look for the ticket for a new one. That is history. Do it. Never look back to the movie you left. All our successful kings had short memory, especially on their failure. Learn from them and capture your history.

When large cross sections of nation's citizen cry, it can be an offence, punishable or time for changes. In a welfare state, can our leaders afford the luxury of making her masses on tears? Why its alleviation is not a political agenda? It appears that we need perpetual poverty to celebrate the freedom of minority, the powerful. This subject is also worth probing. World bodies and judiciary may like to guide our leaders to introduce befitting laws. So make history, at the earliest, using the jerking tears before they are banned. And, wait for the new legislations through which you can make the majority giggle, smile or laugh and pocket the likely incentives like production subsidy for film & serial making and even tax concessions in theatres. To be the king, one has to ban and censor the outcome of film/serial production centres. Suckers of the world are aware of the fact. Play carefully; make use of the opportunity to make money and history.

Team building is more possible among those having traits on the art of sucking, because the successful among them are familiar with the art. It is difficult for us the majority, the common man. Therefore, make use of the gene and innovate. If you use your skill on known and well established earlier traits and schools, probability of risk can be larger. Your qualities you should use to build team and innovate. Most of the modern money spinning devices innovated and established in the market reflects the history of those who have novel skill on knowing the likely market demand on user friendly items of mass demand. These are the current trends and reflecting success stories. In railways too we innovate; but at a slower pace. In communication, our innovations are, even on daily; new products and methods are introduced and sold. They are clever business operators. They knew the market pulse, the wants of even the majority, having less money. We are mostly buyers. An attempt to realize the changing market requirement may be better possible, if the suckers in your family are empowered to perform with wider access to market. Look to your own merits at home, identify those with the skill, aptitude and coronate. You can climb, making history through market operations. It is of late, fashionably permitted. Winners can earn money and governments will recognize with awards, and you can be in history.

Suckers, by nature are bit more self-centred. They don't attribute much value on their family. They are pleasure loving and less caring. This can invite trouble at home. They may bring unexpected troubles to your home when they are on pleasure loving. It can break your dreams and often your family as an institution. You are likely to be mad and can be on the run. Terrorism or Tsunami like devastation can be pushed at home due to the suckers. As a history maker, be conscious more on the breed at home than in your neighbourhood. If available, use their skill in favour you in market operations. The skill is worth for wealth creation and therefore, worth appreciating. Don't waste time on renaissance, reformation, self-meditation or running into woods as earlier we had done. They are less suitable for the occasion and not saleable in the market you are exposed. Always remember that you are on history making, the nation's larger and future history makers. And your time and resource are both scarce and limited. Therefore, use them for your own mission and welfare. Ward yourself from being sucked and thrown out in waste bins as happened early, in the available history. The very realization of suckers will empower you. They are at home. Make use of their skill for making your future history. The old syllabi were drawn by the minority in their favour and to trap you. We valued them and they entrapped us, the majority, with no history. If you are still in doubt, try to recall your great grand father's name, occupation and the physical things they had left for you. Make attempts to trace your own roots. It is worth empowering to work for your future history. The art of sucking is a human trait and it is available at home. Make use of the skill for market intervention and make history. The process will enable us to have appreciable future history.

Episode 7

Brain, Brawn and Behaviour

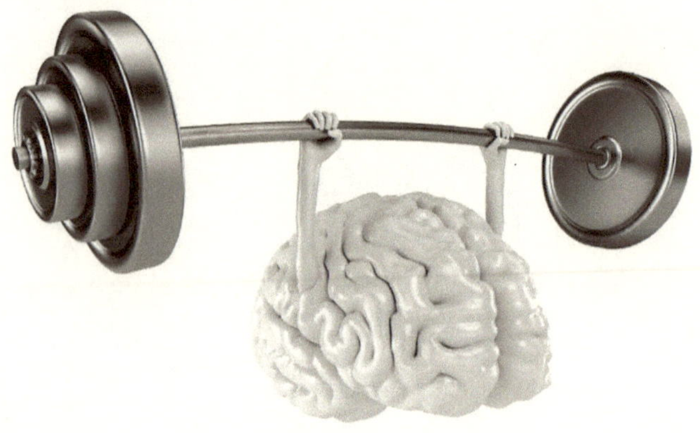

7.1 Brain

It is there in our skull. We style our hair and uplift our look. It is a Trillion-dollar business with new pet names like Saloons, Parlour, Beauty & Health Care Centres and a variety of products and innovative services. Majority of us spend our hard earned money for improving our look and for better showcasing ourselves. Even while combing our hair, we don't become aware of or appreciate the existence of our brain. We have a culture to use it, but not to acknowledge its existence. Brain, is mostly taken for granted. May be because, the minority who make use of the majority, needed our brawn, the muscle, not the brain. They taught us to neglect the item and to a large extent, they were successful inducing fear. As a result, we the majority have relatively less traceable history on the use of our brain.

In the recent past, there are indications on changes. Still fear haunts us. One in the majority, asked an intellectual, 'Guru, if we all together spit on to the colonial rulers, won't they drown in it'? Guru smiled and said, 'By the sight of them, you swallow and run for life'. The communication reflects elements of change and the implanted fear preventing the use of brain.

Use of brain is less acknowledged by us, with no history. We are tuned to forget our own body parts, creativity, skill on memory, computing and even love making. As a result, we are yet to develop market required skill matching with the time, using our brain. Even the wild instinct like rape, appears due to our sheer ignorance to use our brain to trigger and attract even the most demanded personal product or service, love and sex. These are basic subjects a developing market could address to create social values for emerging as civilized set of people in the global market and to attract investors. In any part of the globe, where rape is common, normal investors may not be interested to bare the risk. I often wonder why our Corporates are not interested in making T.V. serials on such subjects. Make use of such market potentials and create history. History can be better possible, with innovation. Earlier, it was possible through invasion, capturing, looting and raping. Replace the gene with innovation, accessing market, making money and using market for enjoyment, creating assets and handing with skill, faith and trade mark for next generation. Our own captains had done it early. And, if you make effort to study them, your brain will open up like the flash-back in commercial film.

We are similar to the wild beast we see in T.V. Even if their flocks are in thousands they can't face a cat. Their body is tuned to run. Similarly, if a reader feels pain to realize between these lines, better close the book and meditate like our loving *Rishi Valmiki* who was designed to terminate in an ant-pit leaving his own people one of the most backward in world history. Never forget the fact that you made history for others as per their desire. It can be a myth. But, it is with us. Shunt the trait and make your own history. Use *Rishi Valmiki* as your brand in corporate world. Be with the wind and fly.

We are yet to open up the brain. Let us first realize its existence. At least while combing, you give a pat to your skull and say, "Yo! mighty brain, hello how are you? We had a rich earlier history of our own people sitting and concentrating, using our brain. The school of yoga, the mighty tool on self-realization and enlightenment are products still saleable. Along with shift in our earlier culture, we were forced to forget the art of even its recognition, realization, use and its powers. We, of late, use them to carry loads. Trade Unions and leaders of head load workers, thereby emerged. Our schools on empowerment of brains are yet to emerge. In that place, schools on empowering muscles became dominant to create fear, conquer and marginalize the majority. During the course of it, the majority were forced to forget the very existence of brain in them. Like for the drug addicts, rehabilitation is painful and we avoid its rejuvenation, the brain was just another head load.

The process of activating brain, was even celebrated by the majority, the common man - presently no history. In the new order, they were reduced as watch dogs resulting its slow termination. They collectively threatened their own ward erring the discipline even pouring boiling lead in to their ears. In the due course, they could make our brain inactive. The result of their brain work was equivalent to cruelty, thy victim here is the majority; with no history. They made us an army of stupids as we were used to make history for them. It is only with the help of colonial rulers we could initiate revitalization of our dead body part, the brain. Our modern schools are their gift. How far we use them to empower our brain is a large subject. We have to thank the British in our opening up. Even, I scribble this note due to their help. My father was not allowed to study at a local school. He had to seek basic education in Ceylon, present Sri Lanka leaving his God's Own Country, present Kerala. The land perhaps still belongs to only of Gods; and not of the people.

Under the new order, globalization, the youth are under forced migration from God's Own Country for sustenance of his family and even for feeding the Gods. We are designed to bear the burden like the loving Christ. Use your brain and realize the fact. Time has changed. Those earlier smart are already in the market making both money and history using their brain; and even hiring the brainy available in your home. If you still use your muscle, make sure that you are not misused. You can be the one still trapped in the old bus. Use your brain and carefully deboard this bus to zombie land.

If I'm misguiding you, look at your own house. Your own near and dear still reflect the inbuilt incapability. We admire girls and ladies with lush hair. How many of us, the history less, admire our own girls using their brain? We continue to be the third rate idiots to follow the script and continue to stamp or enslave them. Please do not forget the old dictum: 'no female eligible for freedom'. In Indian sub-continent, earlier it was practiced under the divine *Manusmrithy*. The merits on practicing slavery are of late, institutionalized under the new names and new forums like religious fundamentalism. But at home, it is much closer to our chest. We the majority, without history, is less comfortable in using our brain. We get uncomfortable like something is thrust down our throat. Realize the inbuilt disorder and change. It is nothing but cultural shift or the well-known old Cultural Revolution. Make it at home. You are free to address and celebrate. That is history making. Liberalize your brain. Allow your loving daughter to use her brain. You will have better sparkling grand children. This guarantees your future history.

For illustration, I share my own experience. In the recent past, I was at my elder sister-in-law's house and chit-chatting with her newly graduated son in Mechanical Engineering. I told him to try for management schools facing competitive exam. His mother was not comfortable. She physically dragged out her son from the scene to avoid the likely intellectual raping. Majority of us are having limitations to visualize the fruits of such changes. Even under the changing scenario, we are yet to touch, taste, feel and address changes. It is difficult to build faith with the majority with anything unknown to them. For ever, they have pulled down their shutters of their brain. They may pretend to listen. But, the No Entry sign tagged on them by the minority, they still love to hold and even adorn them. For them, it is the reality and it is the law at home. Only time and the Brain can break open them.

We are always busy. So we don't have time and we prove ourselves incapable to address changes. If you feel you have brain, it is better to keep away from them and perform. A few will definitely follow smelling, hearing, tasting and even bite on your success stories and enjoy. To make history, keep away from the wild school of thoughts, their practitioners and lovers. You may be alone. But initiate and set a new trend at home. You will emerge as history maker using your brain. This appears as the only way available to the majority, the history less, to make their future history. Beware; I'm addressing a subject only of the majority, those having no history, that is my target group. This is not applicable to the minority, the powerful with history. For you, it can be another entertainment or spark of a silent change. Tolerate, watch and enjoy under the canopy of globalization. You will be shocked to see large set of performers creating history. A fabulous show; like fireworks in a clear sky.

The bloody brain is non-sympathetic to the majority. Look into a classroom with 30-40 children with a product mix of the majority and a few minorities. They are just kids. Yet the brain is blessed with a selected few. In all the gatherings, this is visible. We are tuned to accept the fact. But, why we should lie down and accept a theory made for us? That theory to me is obsolete. If the brain of the majority is a dump, how the educational institutions are mushrooming in the market? Those are the evidence of breaking of the earlier theory thrust in to our mind for enslaving and exploiting us. It is the time for the majority to open up their brain like the world market. Open up your brain. Children should encourage parents in the opening up ceremony. Even Sundays can be used for such small functions at home. Sit together and rediscover your brain, if possible before a lighted lamp. Start thinking how the lamp has encroached in your privacy? Long ago it was lit for empowerment. Subsequently, it was put out by the powerful and often lit for enslaving. Use your brain for breaking the trap. The lamp is well there. Light it. It is your own culture. Shed the imposed and own your culture. That is change. That is history making. Internalize.

In place of the old warding off (sin, spirit, ghost etc.) ceremony, replace with brain opening/strengthening ceremony. Come out from the inhibitions and be better friendly with children who are better exposed to the market and its change. Realize the reality that you too have the priceless asset, the brain which can be opened up, strengthened and used. Along with the known practices, initiate a few new and sail along with the wind, the market forces. Time will never stop for you and I, if we fail to make advantage of the market using our brain. We will be swept away in the wild winds, leaving no history. Our sad old history can again repeat.

Computers have empowered us to have added huge intangible space and thus provided capacity to our brain, to experiment, especially with innovation. Earlier, lot of space we had to use for memorizing, computing, storing and retrieving information, data, their analysis and even history recording. Now, computers can assist us in a large quantum of work. We can therefore, find space in our brain for innovative thinking, research and action and market intervention. Any thinking process of the majority, the history less, is to be market led. Or, there is larger probability to repeat the process of marginalization. Market is the new bus. Use the brain and flourish in the market.

I request the majority to find money to buy computers and install at home, use them and earn an income with it. Earlier, 50 years from now, it was literacy. Now, it is computer literacy. In the absence of the same, the inferiority complex will enter in you and in your child. Treatment for it will be much costly than buying a computer. The instrument will enable your brain to get activated. In a few states in India, computers are given to school students free of cost. It is a great investment on activating human brain and to realize and reach the rest of the world and its ever widening market. Install computers, use them and make history. Encourage the poorest of the poor nearby you, to use smart phones. You are empowering them. You are making them inclusive. The minority with history may smile on their growing market on computers. But watch out, the fast changing technology the majority is likely to bring in. If you are not updated, you have all chance to be knocked out from market without history. There is no 'reservation' and allocation in the market for any. Introduce brain storming at home. If any pull your leg at home, don't hesitate to lock them in their T.V. room. Allow them to celebrate and add to the army of obese and get recycled. Treat it as a part of history making. But never waste your time to drag them to your brain storming exercises. It's impossible and market is not for them. Modernized cemetery will accommodate them; obviously with no history.

7.2 Brawn

As a child, I used to wonder seeing the 'kitten' on the biceps of elder bros. Muscle and musclemen are tradable. In the past, musclemen played a role to make history for others. Often they could also wield powers, marginalizing the brain. Generally, the brain nursed our muscle and muscle power. They deployed them to make their own history. The process often got reversed. However, such incidents had short history. In the long run, the musclemen stood like a waiter in a restaurant to take orders from those with brain. As a segment, they were slaves, enslaved by the brains of others. All killings they have done. The crooks used them to slaughter even the wise men who stood for you, the majority with no history.

If we search for the history of musclemen, we can observe them at home. Still it rules in each institution, right from home. We can observe muscle power at home, on streets, market, religious places, any public gathering, in politics, trade union, education institutions, in films, serials, running buses, trains and even in air craft. Unlike brain power, muscle power loves to show off. In films, directors spent the minimum money on projection of their heroes with muscle. They sell their muscle in male bikini; saving the precious cloths to the needs of the naked; with no history. They market the secret that for making money and history, even bare minimum clothes are not required. These are lessons for the majority to internalize to make money and make history. Most us with no history or short history, attach large shyness to make even muscle a saleable product in the market. Musclemen, who could break the law and capture the market, triggered investments in gymnasiums, providing services and in the production of a variety of healthcare products. It is history. Be in the change process. Be active and make use of the market on muscle power. Muscles are more with us the majority. Don't sell them to the minority. Take them to the market and make history. Use brain and showcase a variety of products and services showing muscle power. Innovate, value add and sell. In your local area itself you may find a virgin market.

Earlier muscle power was used by those with brain to capture all factors of production, viz. land, labour, capital, management and even to optimize their efficiency, often kidnapping champions on efficiency management. Our leaders, judiciary, police and public adore their roles and our agriculture, industry and service sectors thrived once on their muscle power. Law and order are framed by the minority always to use them in their favour. They used musclemen to do what they wanted. Success stories captured due space in history. Right from international terrorism, down to the terror created at home, muscle power and their careful deployment by brain still play significant role, especially for making chaos and mass destruction. National and international, specialized agencies and James Bond films are at market operations, doing, undoing and making history showcasing both reality and fiction. Awards, rewards and punishment are on progress to market the success and failure stories. They make money, using their brain and the muscle. Of late, they even share a part of the surplus to selected musclemen of the majority to deploy their muscle power. A sort of socialistic form of nursing the muscle by the vested interest is at work. The culture is well spread. The scope is wide open to those having no history. Let us also focus on muscle and market. For history making, we have to depend on our own resources. It needs added efforts to reach the market using our brain. But it's worth attempting to address our mission.

Majority of our musclemen end up with no history. But, we had always collaborated with the powerful in taming ourselves and making their history. These qualities are in our genes. Overtime, it has acquired tremendous skill and potential. It is an asset for deployment. We always rented them to the minority using their brain. In a liberalized market, we can sell our assets and its services fully owned by us. We have virtual monopolistic advantage in market. Focus on what we have, use brain and make money in the market and make history. There is less potential on our earlier rowing, carrying palanquins, carrying loads on our head, demolishing and fighting for others, the brainy. If you have no brain, don't worry. Your muscle is enough to explore and conquer in your nearly market. You have the inherent gene tamed for last one millennium. The time is yours. Perform, and make history; capture what you lost. It will enable you to be in future history.

Don't flex your muscle and be law abiding. The market will embrace you. She is bewitching and needs a wide variety like watchmen to studs. The scope is enormous. Invent new use of your muscle; and market. The inherent fear, lust, trust, love, care and compassion can be product-mix worth marketable. Those with history love to get themselves surrounded with the warmth of you, the musclemen. Take care of them and even their belongings. Also, take care of yourself, not to get castrated as had happened in our own earlier history, under our beloved kings and queens. There is much hidden history on the subject worth marketing. Explore and make money.

Like brain, muscles too are also fully owned. It is our luck, the luck of the majority; we still constitute the large supply source of muscle power. Of late, political parties are forced to depend on us and our fully owned supply centres. We too have to be proud of our acquired muscle, knowledge and skill to maintain and tune up them. The brainy, earlier neglected their muscle and concentrated more on developing their brain. Now, there is a shift in their culture. They too want to be fit, firm and flexible. It may be due to the influence of Bruce Lee or Daniel Craig or Would that be Aamir Khan. This shift in preference opens up vast scope for new market and you can flex your muscle there and make history. The above heroes did it. Follow them. If required, make them your heroes or even Gods. But, only use them to make money and make history. Always adhere to the laws, remember the police and the jail. You have limited scope to access market, when in jail. A cultural change is warranted. Address it at least within you and at home. That will ensure your future history.

Under liberalized market, both men and women are liberated and perhaps, women at faster rates. Look at their increasing demand and ensure supply. Many aspire for six-packs. Only in film they are seen. Participate in market operations and ensure the supply. Forget the past. If anything good of you was there, it could have found a place in history. No value to those you didn't inherit or possess. Don't cry on what you missed. Learn to find your asset and be a shrewd market player. You have a pre-history, wherein the brainy could even market goods, services, gods, religious places and develop market around them. If you touch them even today, it will be in top news on ad-papers and watchful media, which they possess. So be careful. Use your education, skill and exposure and launch your products. If necessary, drag the brainy too to the market in launching ceremony. If you are secured with an employment, it is time for you to address the subject. You are under a social security net. Put your hard work and satisfy your boss. But also work for a market led cultural change at home. You should handhold your spouse and kids, when they are in the market to sell.

The social security net will minimize your risk on their market exposure. Find time and tame your muscle as saleable products and acquire new skill and showcase in the market. It's history making. Don't doubt. You're religious by nature. Market is the new order. Be with her; nurse and enjoy. History will emerge. You have seen at least in your T.V. some of our businessmen doing *Lakshmi Pooja*. Follow them; and be in the market with your family selling things, placing the net profit before the deity as King Marthandavarma, in Travancore institutionalized *Thripatidanam*, surrendering the surplus before family deity, and made history with fabulous collection of precious stones, metals and records and warding away from the looters over centuries.

Never forget the fact that you are one among the majority, yet to enter in history. And, you are on history making, using your fundamental rights and subject to the laws of the land. You are also using your own acquired assets, the strength of your body, earlier bonded, now fully owned, but, yet to be patented. Realize the strength in you. Almighty also desires the same. Make use of the exclusive gift he has given to you. Be obliged to Him. Follow King Marthandavarma and take care of your asset the brawn and use it with care to make future history.

7.3 Behavior

It is less noticed by self and more by others. It is marketable, and therefore, need modulations; especially for market operations. We are often welcomed by the smile of a sales person. Perhaps, you were also charmed by a sales person at least once, and you obliged. They are a set, trained on the subject. We majority remain untrained, less refined and therefore, raw material. We talk about 'behave yourself';

but less we attempt to refine ourselves. The subject itself has market potential to make money in near future. During colonial period, there was new trend on mannerism, behaviour and setting habits. From available history, we can easily trace our own behaviour pattern and its changes, especially degradation. Our behaviour is a subject of constant change; and therefore, dynamic. It can be modelled or styled. A cursory look on the subject, appears worth and timely for those interested in getting into the market and making their own history.

Mans' action and reactions are modulated and settled in him as behaviour and its set pattern. Unknowingly, each one of us has a behaviour pattern specific to us. Even in darkness. Europeans' behaviour may be different from those of Asians, Africans or Chinese except when drowning. Similarly, there can be difference in behaviours of sellers and buyers, patients and doctors, peasant and soldiers, young and the elder. In the present analysis, we will confine the pattern of behaviour of the majority, interested in history making in the scenario of the market operations; using market for history making. If you are still at wilderness, I am helpless.

We, the majority are less friendly and very less market friendly. Realize the fact and change. There is a much more dangerous trait in us, we don't allow our near and dear to be friendly with those even within the family and neighbourhood. Over time, we developed many taboos and we tag them proudly due to ignorance. To hide the complex, we often quote our less known scriptures. It is an escape or cowardice; realize and change. Also help your loved ones in their attempts to change. We hear the market is opened. But, we remain ourselves closed. If we wait for the devil or the fate to reach us in our opening ceremony, we are likely to run out and die before making history. It is obviously not our goal. Making history is our goal and therefore, wearing a jersey is like modulating our behaviour. We are to be players and not spectators. We had a history of one in the audience, clapping and cheering performers; history makers. Now time, fate and role have changed. We are in the market to perform, and therefore, we must set right our behaviour. It has to be market friendly.

Our dress code enables us to modulate our behaviour. A swimmer is a misfit in three-piece-suit, similarly, a judge in bikinis. We, the majority are yet to be in love with our dress code. It is not price and time which make us the less reachable. It is the attitude led by ignorance. It needs changes. Proper dress codes of yours will handhold you to have better behaviour. Watch out a brother of ours spitting and pissing in a bus station located in a small township. Watch the same person's behaviour in a modern railway platform and at aircraft terminal. He behaves differently, in each situation. Behaviour, thus, has an influence on our infrastructure. We have limitations for improving common infrastructure. But, we can attempt on our dress code and make ourselves better presentable to reflect our behaviour. Address drastic change at home. Home is also an infrastructure. It is ours and we can address change. Our own set behaviour remain age old; that too shaped by the powerful, the minority. Break them and showcase your inherent better behaviour and celebrate. Be well dressed at home and also showcase your home till the passer by stop and watch at least for a second. Such conscious change in presentation and behaviour will be confidence building and rewarding. It's also an investment in making money and making history.

We have many bad manners and skill on negative marketing. From childhood, we develop a skill on negative marketing, a bad behaviour of ours. We still are proud of such skills and do negative marketing even through popular shows through established T.V. channels. The CEOs of such channels focus the reach; the ugly among us; the majority and they make money and celebrate. Such CEOs are much in demand. Entrepreneurs catch them with high pay and perks. They emerge as champions of negative marketing of our bad habits. These are sets of highly skilled people, but spending more time in their toilets. They thrive, knowing the fact that their viewers don't use their brain and need television to socialise with. Realize the fact that they are our enemy. They highlight our bad manners and make us laugh at our own weakness at our cost. It is negative marketing. Our strength is purposively hidden by this minority. And they live on our earnings like bed bugs, the suckers. We can help them to realize their mistake by disconnecting the cable, say, for 3 months. Make them cool. That is also a way to be in your future history.

Negative marketing is more among the majority having no history or short history. In my school days in a classic regional film, I remember a shot – father asking son – 'son, you failed or passed in X^{th} school exam?' It is a true reflection on our behaviour in negative marketing. We often love to talk on poor health, poverty, misbehaviour of the family members, stories on our liking and disliking. It is our behaviour; and it is in our blood and somehow internalized. Such limitations make innumerable hurdles on our daily life and those initiators in market operations. The set behaviour of ours chops the limps of our jumpers. Realize the limitation, it is cleverly induced in our 'rich' past and they left us in lurching. We had teachers much earlier to guide us. But they were killed, their institutions demolished and even memories and remains stamped under mud. It is worth excavating to discover ourselves and change our behaviour. This will help us to shift from the prevailing negative marketing of ourselves and our own near and dear.

Behave yourself. Come out of the fetters of those implanted behaviour. Those are the dirty habits still left in you. Open toileting among us, the majority, is a 'proud' behaviour. A researcher tells that the history less will not sit on a platform their own elderly sit and shit. So the young, including daughter-in-laws squat on the side of the roads and stand and hide their face forgetting their bottom to avoid flash light of motors rarely poke on their roads. It is a classical behaviour on negative marketing of the youth by the elderly stupid. Even their proud elders can't remember the names of even their forefathers. But, they pose themselves as guardians of a paid history. Their behaviour, they project divine as above, at the cost of their daughter-in-laws bottom on flash light, a typical negative marketing. I have seen it, not once, but many times during my visits to local areas on official duty. Open your eyes. You can witness the royal behaviour of ours despite the national level call on cleanliness. Change the behaviour.

We have an extra ordinary skill to take things light. We fail to behave ourselves except in a few occasions like death, unforeseen incidents, marriage or child birth. Such occasions we have a set behaviour, institutionalized. We, having no history, are more proud on our behaviour. A few of us often create a scene in the above occasions and make the situation worse. It is negative marketing, perhaps due to ignorance and lack of exposure on the new market. Or, someone has taught us wrongly. Our behaviour in such occasions make a mess of things around and we celebrate even indulging in word wars, fist fight, or running away from the scene. Should we continue such nasty behaviour? The youth only can handle them. If necessary, drag them to the market, showcase the primitive behaviour and make your history.

Our females have a set in behaviour due their specialization on food making, child care, cleaning, warming up our home and surrounding. Along with time, a variety of labour saving devices have minimized their drudgery. As a result, there is sizable leisure, especially for those at home. With their acquired behaviour, a few focus on to further warm up their own homes; and the rest often fumes family members out from their own home. Such behaviour has an increasing trend and further institutionalization through the visual media. Through such unfortunate behaviour, we are also emerging in the market as champions of family breakers. Channelling the extra energy of house wife appears to have large scope for market intervention. Address the subject and make money. There is scope for innovation and to make use of the newly created surplus energy.

Unused energy is inflammable like LPG cylinders and a few of our homes are currently under fumes. There can be mounting pressure due to our own neglect in using the energy gained. Wrong channelling results in obese and negative marketing. We may hesitate to own the emerging behaviour. But, their wild growth is due to our own neglect. We miss an internal system for timely correction. Our market is more on treatment and less on prevention.

In their absence, self-awareness and self-addressing are the current alternative. The time-lag in addressing will result in a variety of family and social issues. The process has opened up new avenues on money making business in wine shops, new shelters for young and old. If you are helpless in behaving yourself, at least make use of the opportunity and be market friendly; make money and be in history. If we are unable to behave ourselves and make our own history, be ready for exploitation as happened in the past. History repeats. New scope for exploitation can emerge in the market. So Take care. Be market friendly and make use of the opportunity and change. Take care of the market trend and guard yourself so that you don't stand on queue to fill in their cash box. Reverse the process and make history.

Episode 8

Leg Pulling, Hand Folding and Hand Holding

8.1 Leg Pulling

We spend more energy on pulling leg. Overtime, we have developed special skill on the same. In poli-tricks, it is our national unification factor. From time immemorial, we have role models on the subject. Our ad-papers and ad-medias allocate more time on debating about leg pulling. Leg pulling is a part of our culture; a national hobby. Of late, it appears to be more with the poor climbers on the steps of history. The minority once upon a time was too good on the trait.

Perhaps, reduction of their size to microscopic minority, newly established system of inheritance of both money and power by siblings; and the increasing opportunity on money transfers to banks etc. may be favourable factors resulting in low level leg pulling among the powerful, the minority. Perhaps, they might have reached better consensus among themselves and minimized the risk involved in pulling the legs of others especially those at par with them.

A friend of mine believes that leg pulling is inborn like gravitational pull. Instead of the great pull to centre of the earth, we the majority, pull down to the floor and stamp our partners and co-players in mud. We have hidden history pulling down our own teachers; forcing them to bear heavy burdens and making them run for their life. Like the mother earth, we also pull the leg of the one near to us. In space, it doesn't work. We don't like taking a passport, stamping a visa, spending on travel and pulling someone at a distance. We especially the weak, love to pull the nearest. The game starts at home. More powerful may extend the art to neighbourhood, work places and places we assemble and the strongest dreams to make it continental. But, they rarely practice, due to fear on extinct.

Among the majority, leg pulling is self-learnt and practiced. The art of team work is currently limited to those wielding power. In history, there were schools and champions on leg pulling. But, they practiced the art to safeguard their own vested interest. They thought it divine to pull others leg for their own survival and to safeguard their laws they marketed under scriptures and through myth. In those periods, the majority were onlookers. Of late, we too inherited or acquired the skill and also practice and express our freedom. For testing our skill, we start practicing at home. The timid among us first pull the legs of our spouse; then our own parents and kids. The inbuilt timidity limits our scope for expansion. We all are kings riding our own horses at home. When we ride, we venture to pull down the weak and then even the horse. The result is predictable. That's our history and somehow we love it.

The set practice continues. We are yet to learn to gallop together taking care of the horse, the family and joy of the royal pleasure. Our urge for the different pleasure, makes us pull our own legs. We are notorious in pulling down our co-riders, our spouse, parents, kids, teachers and the hand holders. They are our enemy. We are kings. We need enemy for our own kingly existence. Pulling legs is an inborn trait and a martial art. As kings, we have to wage wars. If there is no place outside; why can't we practice and perish at home? Who beliefs in history? We lived thousands of years without it. But those were time; others pulled our leg en masse. Now we are in majority, with freedom and with no history. Let us pull our legs and perish. Let history repeat. We are better civilized; and let us perish in our own mighty culture by pulling the leg of the nearest. The process, be careful, leaves you with no history, like our earlier Rajas, the petty Kings. Just opposite is our current mission. Don't forget. Can't we come out of the old stupid kingly traits? You were never a king. Then why you want to be one when the tribe itself is dead and gone due to their mutual leg pulling.

Others' fall, we enjoy. It gives us instant pleasure. During earlier time, there was no entertainment at home, other than those family could provide. Now, cable takes care of the space and 24 hours we are entertained; often, on the joy of leg pulling. Yet, we love to practice the art. It is our habit and culture. In metros, people rush and they have less time on the art. But at home, who are at leisure, we have to practice. And, they do practice the art sincerely. Many practitioners of the art pose innocence. When caught, they say they act childlike. But, take care of yourself, or else, they can make your chest as their score board. We have these innocent devils with us. They have destructive attitude and powers. They never build anything and proud of themselves as suckers or destroyers. If you fail to ward them, they can destroy what you make. You are more exposed, when they are at home. Like you enjoy building, they derive pleasure in destruction of what you make. It is a direct attack and not like the terrorist you are familiar with. Their actions are much predictable. Whereas, the action at home or at your work place is unpredictable and it can make you doom and without history.

Watch out the leg pullers around you. There is no much use in listening to national or international news on the media. Find time to look around you to save yourself from leg pullers. If you are smart and a likely history maker, the leg pulling can start at the very nascent stage at home, in your carrier or business. I have experienced the long spoke of their schools planning 30 years in advance to check my carrier climbing process. If you are likely to be a threat to the invasion in their history and growth, they will definitely pull down your leg. It's their *Dharma*, divine duty. These schools have many tools, both direct and indirect. After identifying your liking and disliking they will act even, nursing, caring and finally leg-pulling. The art is so smooth like a close shave in a saloon or a face lift at a beauty parlour. They are good at their work. They enjoy the work and also enjoy your fall. Unlike you, they don't feel any guilty conscious. It is as said above, is their *Dharma* as believed by them for the last

1000 years. So, internalize an art to save yourself. Only with your skill, you can have success and make your own history.

If your home has vacant space, leg pullers can even penetrate from outside. They are shrewd and therefore, they have confidence on their skill. You have to keep them at a distance, if you work for success in your life. We majority have a limitation in keeping secret. We feel proud and empowered when secret is shared. The listener also has the same weakness and they too share your secret and emerge as your leg pullers not as confident keepers as you see in your T.V. or read in a text. If you feel like telling the secret to your dearest, never make the mistake. Your first axe may fall from them chopping your planning process. Keep them guessing. When your crop matures, you can think of opening up of your market. Or else, they will uproot your baby plants. It's fun for them. You may pardon them as if due to their curiosity. But, realize the fact that they are designed to do it as a *Dharma*. That is the success of the earlier culture, the powerful taught. So take care, if you are a history maker. Never allow others to expose your roots. It'll get sun dried.

Of late, modern instruments are available to practice the art on leg pulling. Take care of the audio, video, micro devices like hidden cameras and the packed food and gift. If you are a performer, your surroundings can be potential market for these devices. Your careless and friendly sharing of information and images can result in pulling your legs. Your own ignorance on the use or misuse of these products can pull your own leg and can be trapped like the reverse firing pistols you see in James Bond films. You pull the trigger and you perish yourself. A relative of mine, kept a hidden camera used for surgical purpose at home and he lost his family seeing unpleasant things. He was successful in pulling his own leg, in-spite of his education. He missed his homely bus. It is due to the inborn culture and wrong use of James Bond's pistol. You are taught to tear off your own history. Take care. And, never pull your own legs. You have only two feeble legs. How can you afford to pull even one, when you are at history making?

The strings of your heart are yours. Don't share with any. Learn the art from your female partners. They chat a lot on others, but they don't make any sounds on themselves so that others can pull their leg. Share only the essential with the players and even with prospective players. They may pull your leg and make you sick and keep you out. There is no rule on earth that you weaken yourself so that others can ride on you. In earlier days, our activities were limited to meet basic necessities. Now, it is global market and you are an aspirant to participate. For history making, the above tips are essential. Even to sell this book, I have to be innovative and market savvy. Or else, I will be pulled down in the market with torn purse.

Leg pulling remains yet to be recognized as a tradable service in the market and empower its practitioners and protect the likely victims. If it is a game, it could have emerged in market. Even prostitution is a recognized age old service. Then, why not leg pulling? If necessary, we may rechristen or rename the service to suit the current corporate culture. Each one of us is having lust, yet we fail to recognize it; as if the subject is too personal. But the art of leg pulling, I feel is better market led. Often, we use it as a hidden tool in capturing new markets and conquer the rivals and competitors. Many stories and films on the subject we witness. But, rarely a book giving guidance or an agency specialized in the art and rendering services is yet to emerge. Detectives and secret services in private sectors only could peep on the subject. It is perhaps limited to research or to trigger the thinking process to achieve corporate objectives. For the majority, like us, the subject remains amateur. To me, these are avenues for new business. Take care of the likely and existing threats on the art. If you are at your own climbing process, take care of the likely hurdles and guard yourself. You can have better probability of success rates in history making if you are alert.

8.2 *Hand Folding*

Hand folders are ladies and gentlemen. They are a set of law abiding, well dressed and soft spoken. They love peace and keep themselves away from activities at home and neighbourhood. They are more like spectators in a play often rushing in, watching, cheering and enjoying. When an accident takes place, they will rush, watch and disperse. They will never get themselves involved in any happening. They are not selfish or harmful. Even they will fold their hands and watch their own life. They hesitate to perform. Perhaps, their genes are like that. None can change the traits.

Hand folders are everywhere. We can watch them at home, work places, gatherings and in crowd. They constitute a sizable and they are alive in the market. Market operators meet their demand and make money. A few of them are proud of their role. They feel themselves privileged. If necessary, they fight for their legitimate claims and enjoy life. They are hygienic in nature and always prefer to showcase themselves even at the cost of others. They don't feel guilty for the same.

Compared to the rest in the majority, less familiar about their own history, hand folders are better informed on the subject we deal with. Often, they are proud of their history and love to project the selected stories on them and dark part of others. They project themselves as knowledgeable; but keep away from any physical work. When need arise, a few of them even cook up new stories, often predict the future and draw people's attention.

In history, they played roles like messengers, opinion seekers, go between, news canvassers and disseminators. They are not ambitious. They are conscious on the short length of their life and they love to enjoy life not doing hard work. They also don't like to take any risk, make adventures or participate in market. They love to remain in history, but feel incapable and fold their hands and watch the same.

Check your own status. If you are identifying yourself as one among them, don't be unhappy. We constitute a sizable and there is no worry on our history. Someone will allow us to get in to their vehicle. Take care, you board in time. A large group of us were always in the segment of the leftover. A new vehicle reached us 2500 years back; and, only a few of us ventured to board. Others were left out. Then nearly 700 years after, another vehicle reached us at high speed drawn by horses and carrying arms made of steel. Among the left over and from the earlier vehicle a few smart jumped in. They kicked those running behind the fast moving vehicle. A large number missed both the buses and watched the show. They remained there without change. They are those not included; and, we call them aboriginal.

From such happenings, we might have inherited the gene on hand folding. It is not forced folding. It is self and natural, a trait of our own. A sizable among us, the history less, still prefers to fold our hands watching those performing. The culture is internalized. Now, new school of thoughts calls out for inclusiveness. Unfortunately, they still constitute the majority, without history. Realize your status; and think, why you miss in current history? If you realize the reason, jump into the new vehicle, the market, right at your door step; and, make your future history. Never fold your hand.

Hand folders are better consumers. We can sell goods and services to them. They will manage money. They have added skill on flicking money like your loving younger brother. They have a unique skill on money management. They never become bankrupt. Take care of yourself, the history makers for achieving your goal. A few of them, also have added urge in market exclusively for buying new products and services. They like to show off through periodical face lift, switching over to the new fashions, travelling, celebrating and adapting better technology like computers and smart phones. They are a large market and you history makers can make use of them. Make them up to date. Through prospective business a change in culture can be aimed at during the course of our history making.

Take care not to initiate any direct investments or services to change our attitudes. We are like sea sands. We will not bind ourselves. Realize our limitations; but make use of our large army. History records bitter experience on the attempts to change our traits. We can force them to shift space, faith or traits; but, not by persuasion. The change may take place but at a slow pace. How far it will fit into the fast changing market is a subject for those concerned on future history.

Hand folders, as a large segment is God-fearing. They love to present themselves in their best folding their hands and enjoying. Look at a small function at home. They will definitely ensure their presence and make you happy. But they will not participate in any of your efforts to organize the function. A few of them will also criticize you in private before fully digesting the food they enjoyed. Parents love to see their children prosperous. Hand folders are no exceptions. They too have ardent desire on the success of their wards. But a parent under hand folders will never act. They are helpless. They can simply wish. If both the parents are in the same school, then you can well predict the future. Focus on your homely traits and adopt suitable strategy and make history.

Match makers, use horoscope as a tool to avoid the likely risk in marriage. In history, frequent use of the services of astrologers and match makers can be observed. Of late, use of computers for instant match making are in vogue. For successful sustenance of the family, history makers might have used their skill to minimize the risk in avoiding the match of two good hand folders, like a shrewd captain or umpire selecting their players to ensure the much wanting success of his team.

Based on self-assessment, you find yourself the setting at your home. Never make an attempt to deceive yourself. Each trait has its own merit. Focus on your strength and others within the family. On better realization of your own traits, and sharpening skill, you will be able to make use of your own family as a team to make history. As time is scarce, don't venture to tame any; including yourself. It is a long driven process and unaffordable especially in the new bus. So, focus on your marketable traits and initiate change process. That will ensure you to address your mission, future history.

8.3 *Hand Holding*

This is a rare trait. A few of us of course have genes on handholding self and others, especially those nearer to us. They have skill on the subject and the much required will too to perform. You may visualize a person drowning and another saving him voluntarily. He/she is the hand holder. They possess the skill to swim and the much wanting urge to save the one being drowned. They are obviously history makers. Often, they too are crucified like the story of a youth who saved the life of a rich feudal girl dying in water. After saving the dying girl, he was killed by the arrogant and ignorant. The story is filmed and marketed. Hand holders can be martyrs like Gandhiji and Martin Luther King. So, watch out and perform taking care and enjoying life. There is no need for sacrifices to make future history.

Hand holders are change agents. They are at our home. We don't like to recognize and acknowledge them. Often, our own children set new trends at home and attempt to hold our hand from the beaten track. Realize the fact and be considerate to accommodate such aspirations at home. If you nib them from their very bud due to ignorance, you are blocking your own way to the set of history makers. The king in you can often roar at such initiator at home and block them on a subject you feel alien. The faculty on handholding is a must to build team spirit. Our kids initiate the subject while playing with other children. Kindly not disturb them. If you have an urge to rule, channel your energy to your loving spouse. You have limited energy at any point of time. Use it to conquer new horizons of love, care and compassion with the spouse and build your home. If you're a history maker, please leave the children and conquer your spouse. Allow the child to make history for you and together, you handhold your loving kids to be in future history. Try sincerely. It's possible. That'll change your history.

The supply of hand holders is limited due to the parent's poor background to shape their own children's gene. When the supply lags, scope for emergence of a new breed will occur. Hand holders emerge through experimenting, exploring, learning and enabling the near and dear to perform and perfect. It needs time and energy to play with. This can't be moulded or trained in management schools. We are ignorant on hand holders and their make. As a result, we try to stamp them as sometime volunteers, a few clubbed under Non Govt. Organizations or those rare specimens in the vast army of various trades and services. People love them; and they love to record them in history. Those who happened to be in power and reflected handholding become heroes of their time. Of late, a few occurrences under this phenomenon can also be observed under new wave films and even in politics. It is a welcome change to create history, especially for those leftover.

Hand holders role in a family and in a local area is yet to be realized, recognized and supported. Currently, only top heroes steal the show. Our school education and teaching system are partially responsible for the neglect, like our family units. Along with the current teaching, teachers are to be hand holders. Excepting a few, majority of the teachers are executing only their job matching with the stipulated minimum requirement. The larger objectives to handhold those future performers are on the back bench of their priority list. Majority of the teachers suffer from the complex of knowing all about and beyond which nothing existed. Such teachers have the mighty school of limited thoughts on mother earth and the social issues on her surface. Most of them are on their adolescents and not having a concept on history beyond, say beyond their own drawn surroundings. They appear happy with their limiting factors. They have limited counting ability. Such bench marks often limit their faculty on handholding. They talk less on freedom and more on discipline and love to discipline future generation, their students, as if it is their prime duty. Entry into unknown areas like handholding is less encouraged by the management and initiators often warned and punished. For imposing discipline, fear is created in the minds of the young by which students initiatives are often killed.

The managers of the school, during my time, walked on school compound wielding long canes, creating terror to tame us. For them, we were wild beast in the campus till the long bell during evening hours. Then they relax and their battery is to be recharged to rule the next day. They could rear their inborn qualities in school campus. They could never practice love, care, compassion or to develop a faculty on handholding, building faith and team work. We missed these things during our school days. How they could miss the loving smiles of our great Teachers is a question still haunts me even today. Canning was common. Pissing in our knickers when caned was much common. I had to witness even chaining my classmate within the class room. His sad face still haunts us. The much wanting LOVE we missed during the long 10 years we were in our school. Unfortunately, it was the best school in our town. Situation might have obviously changed; and, today's youth are better blessed. But take care. We miss the basic lessons on the art of hand holding. For making history it is essential.

Only during school inspections by higher authority, our management thought of building team work to project us and please them. The slaves in them, made use of such tricks for continuation of slavery. Teachers were a tribe, dead and long gone with their genes due to the long impact of the Dark Age extending the past one millennium. Presently, timidity and fear can be observed more among them. They pose themselves well-disciplined and restrict their students within the syllabi and more within the four walls of their classrooms. Making them aware of the limitation is a herculean task. You can't guide the present teachers. They have a mind set with inherent limitations on self-improvement. Keep away from such futile exercise. You will lose your precious time and limited energy within you. But, realize the limitation of our school education and make use of your inherited skill to develop the faculty of your kids. If you have doubt, stop your vehicle at the side of the road, and ask a teenager about a popular person living around or the way to nearby place. You will get a face mostly blank. It is not because of his ignorance on the person or place, but because of the fear in him on handholding you. If I'm proved wrong, the school is good on empowering their student. If not, you draw your own inference. I don't blame the teachers, they could mostly inherit only fear. One can share only what they have. Hand holding is something new. Picking, sorting, packing and transporting, we know better. So we pick up 2 or 3 smart among the 40 students in a class, project and export them. We get remittance and we like to suck the smart. That is our history, the history of our surrounding. It is time to address change. A new culture on hand holding our loving school teachers should induct. It is obviously out of the current syllabus. Make attempts to know what is available in and around your school. A new faculty on hand holding will emerge; handhold first at your level, then extent to your students. It will ensure better son/daughter-in-law, who will hesitate to burn you alive.

Handholding can play larger role, if initiated by the majority, the history less. Of late, I could witness a change process worth mentioning. In a survey of returnees from Middle East and their entrepreneurial initiatives, I was impressed by a few fishermen who invested their hard earned money in mechanized fishing vessels. They didn't avail bank loan and deploying their own near and dear and internalizing the better techniques they learnt from the fishing sector in host country they could successfully carry out regular fishing operations within a short period. This appeared to me as an extraordinary handholding of the local youth by a technologically savvy new generation of returnee fishermen with better confidence and team building spirits. These are change process worth recording in local history. Instead of availing the services of a conventional fishery officer, can we invite a successful local fisherman and enlighten our students in coastal area on mechanized fishing? For making future history, we have to avail the services of such resource persons. Our teachers can also learn on real fishing operations from them and together they can handhold the students on the subject, especially those come from a coastal area. Under liberalization, our schools too have to open up. Schools are the best place for confidence building and teachers can make wonders in the new scenario.

We should develop a collective will to make use of the locally available hand holders and change agents in all possible local institutions. If we depend on age old systems, we will make no progress in our local area and thereby no history. Such lessons are worth for students of history, and the new history makers. All the poverty alleviation programs throughout the globe have larger failure than success due to their over dependence on such imported resource persons. Whereas a few change agents could make history through addressing group dynamism, introducing appropriate technology and making use of the local area skill, resources and management. Those are history of the hand holders and not of the bureaucrats engaged on touch and vanish, popularly labelled as T & V in less developed area. Poverty continues to survive challenging the merits and skill of those champions. They too perished without history. That is history. Such bitter experience will enable us to learn more on hand holding. Internalize handholding trait first within you and then extend to your family. When matured, handhold at least one of your friends, relatives or a neighbour. It will widen your market. The new culture will ensure the best future history for all of us. Visualize and change. That is Globalization.

<h1 style="text-align:center">Episode 9</h1>

Gains, Realization and Re-engineering

9.1 Gains

We the majority, attempting to make our own future history are to be conscious on our gains: self-gains, family gains, gains of the neighbour. A consciousness on our own achievement, we are yet to realize. This status weakens us. We may possess the minimum required qualities to qualify, but, we miss the faculty to realize the same. As we are less aware of our own gains, we hesitate, withdraw and shy ourselves from showcasing gains. Reasons are many for this situation. That is history, and most of such traits are yet to be observed and analysed. I'm trying to make you conscious on your own gains so that you can better perform in the market, and, not to meditate and find the ultimate truth behind your trait. That is a larger subject. Let us first probe into our more realizable gains for market intervention with the simple objective of making self-history and our future history.

Let us first list out own gains and make ourselves conscious on the subject. Our body, mind and inherited genes is owned by us; and under liberalized current status, these are completely ours. Killing is a criminal offence and therefore, our killers won't attempt directly. Indirect attempts are still there and we have an art of acquired skill on defence and survival. The very awareness on the subject will make us realize better and guard our personal gains. Remember, we are the majority without much gain to be listed and a set of people living even without history. This self-conscious will enable us to search and fill the gap and make history.

So, take care of your person, your body, your mind and other physical items you possess. Don't pledge those things to others; even to the nearby banks. It is reintroduction of the earlier slavery. Time could abolish only its physical form. The attitude to make others slave is still with us. The culture of enslavement and looting still prevails even at our home and at our work place. It is everywhere. So, take care. Otherwise, you will lose your meagre gains and lose your new earnings and precious time for fighting to guard them. When weak, your entry into the market, they will check. Then, you have to be in the market only as a consumer that too if you have money; or, they will push you out as waste. And, your place will be in the newly kept dust bin, with the proud tag, 'Use Me'. That is the new style in the market similar to the earlier religion based social and economic set up. Similar to the present trading on shares in the stock market; our own forefathers were traded in the recent past. If you can find time to look at our history, it will open up a variety of supply sources to further strengthen your gains. Please attempt. That will empower you to further assimilate your gains.

If you are not that wild and emotional, find time to discuss the subject GAIN with your loved one. The process will make you rich and build team spirit at home to realize the assets and liabilities of your family. For the time being, treat the family unit, as an enterprise and you an accountant. It is fun to know your own net asset. Deploy the net for optimum gain. You will make history. You will be a better player, both at home and in the market. Your gains will make you strong, proud, energetic and you will emerge with the 'killer instinct,' advocated in sports & games. The process of tightening, or realizing the gains will make you more fit to perform. It is obviously a new culture for us. Please internalize and change. It's necessary for your future history.

We are generous in under rating ourselves on our gains. This can be observed in our answer to the usual friendly query, 'Hello, How are you?' We prefer to under rate our gains by a casual response like, 'Ok, dragging' or 'Ok, as usual' or *'Chaltha Hai,'* moves on etc. We don't like to say, 'I'm ok and kicking' or I'm doing well and making use of the opportunity'. We are shy to share on our gains. We hide our gains as if the other guy is designed by the Almighty to trouble you. The process, make ourselves covered with our own poor ads. The same guy, when asked about how was the latest movie? The reply can be *adipoly*, excellent, thrilling, fantastic, heart throbbing or boring. We like to market others gains and hide our own gains. Let us realize the fact; and change ourselves. We are on a mighty job; and, never forget our mission – History Making.

Our education, skill and acquired family status are definitely our gains and we are to be proud of them. With the changing time, we should learn to channelize or market our gains. The present culture may not allow us to address the changes. It's moulded by the powerful to make their history. Those were not real history makers. The 'scholars' teach about them as history, leaving us the majority. Such 'scholars' still continue their business to earn their livelihood from the set tradition. Along with time, they will get enlightened and hold the torch on true history to be inclusive in the changing market. In the market, you can't survive cheating consumers for a long time. Cheaters can have short term gains. But their history is also short lived. You have the long genetically gained skill and specializations on various trades. Earlier day's skilled blacksmith are in the list of the rich steel producers in the world today. Similarly, carpenters turned boat and ship builders, gold smith managing worlds' precious metal and diamonds trade, the one started with a bullock cart own and operate the largest road transport service etc. are befitting role models in the change process. We are proud of them. But, we are less proud of our traditional skill. Realize our limitation and sharpen our traditional skill. Through technology up gradation, even traditional products are still tradable in the new markets. Let us love our acquired family skill. It is our strength. Use them, modernize and be in the market. The process will ensure you in history. Those are our real gains; our assets.

Avoid the current habit of not recognizing yourself and your families' values and acquired skill. If you are a traditional farmer and land in your local area is a constraint, locate land where it is available. Migrate, settle, introduce modern farm practices and make history. Explore new avenues for your genes to perform. You need not stick to your current place and sacrifice your own life and bond yourself and your kids. If you search your own history, you can find yourself in the history or details of your forefather's reaching, settling and their efforts to flourish when there was potential. If there are resource constraints, consolidate your gains and resettle in potential areas like the colonist and earlier Aryans, Dravidians, Babylonians, Arabs and of late, the Jews great return to their own motherland. Migrants turned entrepreneurs in Middle East and those returned and set up their enterprises in local areas are history makers right in front of us. Vast potential await you to sow the seeds of development and make history. Once you are on progress on market operations, other vital forces like self-realization and enlightenment will follow you during your mature age. Of late, all services are market led. If you have doubts, scan the current spiritual leaders history; and, you will find them providing their goods and services more in economically well developed countries or regions or platforms were infrastructure and leisure are better available for their event managers to showcase their products and services. We can even learn A to Z market operations from our own current spiritual leaders. They are making a lead and let us sort out our gains and follow them in the market and make success stories; our future history.

If you attempt on accounting process at macro level, you may find the factors of production viz. land, labour, capital, management and efficiency more with the minority wielding power. They have also an advantage to hire labour, the large majority of us, for optimum use of land, capital and even management. We are at obvious disadvantages; and, we should be aware of our own limitation to find us in history. This is a large subject and we shall treat it separately under this episode itself. It is a limiting factor and let us explore to locate the end of the tunnel. Those among us and having skill on probing should focus on the subject. Perhaps, you will be enlightened by your own genes, the great teachers had planted in you. That is one of our gains, yet to be realized. The subject, I place before you to probe and gain. Never dispose the factors of production you currently possess. Acquire skill to make them economically sizable; so that you can deploy them most efficiently and be in history.

9.2 *Realization*

Realization of one's own strength or gain is an art, and we are yet to develop the skill. Earlier, empowerment schools were at work, almost a millennium ago; and reasons best known, we have pulled down their shutters. We shifted from brain to muscle and through the process, we weakened our brain and we were forced to live under fear. For realization of our own strength, we may have to search in our own dark period, the dark tunnel and for the light. Easiest way is to close our eyes and pass through the tunnel and realize our own genes and give them life, revitalize. It is a herculean task for the traditional; and, easy for the youth with the new bent of mind and better market savvy.

If we can realize the dark tunnel in which we are currently trapped; the light also you can find at the very end of it. Be viral and stimulate the rest; the leftover; having no history. It will emerge as a silent revolution in knowing ourselves, our trap, the tunnel, the chocking dirt and dust, the light and ultimately our own gene, the much suppressed over a millennium. None can stop us from this process under current liberalization. Forget the past. Jump over it. Go to the past-past rewind, search and realize yourself. You are bright and illuminated there. To tune up your gene, make your own attempt. If you are savvy, make use of the social media and go global, linking your own leftover. Break the timidity and globalize. In your genes, the much sought after excellence is hidden. Realize. Don't miss the opportunity. We have missed the bus earlier; and, we lost over a millennium. That made us with no history.

The process will open up large canvas on entrepreneurship, access to new factors of production and addressing higher level of productive efficiency. The newly created link with the leftover will make you better market friendly and life worth living. The history on pain, poverty, deprivation, tears and helplessness can be made historical items of the past by you, the history makers. You are a mighty force and realize the same by yourself, your family and your neighbourhood. Lift all shutters, come out and jump over the hurdles. You don't have any history and therefore, be shameless. Conserve your energy and use it to perform in market. Plug leakages, if any. Realization and performance can be our strategy for making our own history. Talk less, think and perform. Ward off the (barking) dogs. They are our own brothers. When changes take place, a new Ram will bless them like Ahalya with *shapa moksha* under a condition 'Work hard and keep shut your mouth'. That will make you to make the new product; your future history.

From the minority, the smart, the well-educated the well trained and the talented reach the market. It is a larger force to reckon with. Those powerful still formulate laws for the majority, having no history, observing the large ears of elephants. The mighty beast is unable to realize the fact that it is the largest mammal on land. The majority, the history less or having short history, are tamed like elephants to carry the heavy burden, and always obstructing it to realize its own strength. For enabling the process, the shroud still cage most us with the tags like touchable, untouchable, caste, creed, tribe, stamping based on colour, shape, region, religion, power, money etc. All are categorized, compartmentalized and chained on duties and to make them unaware of their own strength. The majority, without history, at an elderly age roams like 'King Elephant' in deep woods throwing mud and dust, scratching and itching to die without history. The clever taught us the wrong philosophy of life. And for them, we made monuments, wrote history and sculptured poetic epithet. We were told and retold to get our share from above, where Neal Armstrong could only float and find thick dust. The cake was reserved for the powerful. And, the majority, with no history was taught to get it from Almighty. As taught, we practiced and we got the cake, the mighty Maya; and, they eat the yummy real one. You are designed to adhere to those LAWs even under globalization and liberalization. When they eat cake you get *Moksha*. If you have still patience, please wait in queue.

Others, please get into the market, perform and eat branded cakes; and make history. Leave the sky-high ladder to the heaven to its own designers. You enjoy your life with your near and dear and make future history for your kids. They will ensure your *Moksha*. They are yours and therefore, better reliable. Please realize the fact that market is the new social order, the new social carrier like the earlier religion and you better get into the new bus.

A few among us are still aware of our teachers who taught us self-realization. But, we seldom practice. We feel out of range on the subject and hang up. Presently, we love ourselves to be seen busy. We also take pride in pretending ourselves having no time even for own realization. At home, each one pose busy on the other, especially to those, very near. We make ourselves collective busy and run ourselves. No time to stop; think and realize. As a result, our brain is less cared and it remains less developed. The run make us proud owners of plastered limps. Only in hospitals we find time to realize ourselves and we are destined to munch '*double rotties*,' instead of branded cakes.

In short, someone should break our limps to enable us to realize ourselves. Of late, it has become a fashion. Around us, the humble cats and dogs curl up, realize and enjoy their life. We don't have the time to look upon them and learn. Our planners and administrators also make us run, run for our life. They too run showing off. The work which can be done within 3 hours is stretched for 8 hours. The run is not to address the work and complete in time; but to report to the boss, surrender to the minority, wielding power and to advertise the false identity to keep power. These ignorant make us all run. We are the slaves who slog; and not those efficient at work. It is of late, becoming a culture to make ourselves busy to slog and make us inefficient. Realize the fact and say, good-bye, to the loving boss. Let him find his own person who can daily update him and also scratch on his bottom. You use your head. Let us rejuvenate it. It's realization of your asset and not the bottom. History making is possible only with your head. Realize the fact and make history.

The current days are designed by the powerful due to their own inherent inability to realize what they need. They are notorious to exploit us to cap their own inefficiency. Their rules and regulations are more fit for the wild, and not for the civilized. Instead of realizing the merits and allowing them to perform at their best, the primitive culture of taming them like the beast still persist even under the changing scenario of globalization. Realize the inbuilt limitation. They even will not allow you to realize your own gains, your own talents, skill, specialization and the mighty urge of yours to perform. You are still bonded. It is their mission to check you out from the process of making history. If you could read between the lines of the available baked history, you can observe king makers engaged in production of kings; mini, small, medium and large.

You can also learn the tricks of those kings terminating their own makers including their own papas. In the melee, you can also find when they failed as rulers; and, invaders raped and looted. It is the *Maha* Culture, *Maharaja* Culture they gave to us, especially to the majority; without history. Try to learn from what really happened to you. Realize and protect yourself and make history. Never boast blindly on the earlier 'Proud Culture'. I could search and there is nothing which I could get an ecstasy; may be because of my wrong age. You try. But, realize the fact that Time has emerged as one of the important factors of production in the market. Never waste it. You may have to shed a few conventions to be in the market.

If required, break them. Come out of the cocoon and realize your own merit. Walk towards the market and interact. Develop the desired skill on market operations, like the stock brokers. Make use of the newly available freedom to you and look at your own kids and kin to realize their own merit and potential to perform. Come out of both the ignorant king and the slave in you. Don't rule at home. Conserve energy and get into the market. Realize yourself and showcase your merits. That is history making. In place of the old battle and battle field, it is market and market competition. Realize, perform and be in history. Get out from the old status of diggers of own graves. Forget the bitter past and perform. You will realize your merits and make history.

Never run away from the fact that we have no history and nothing left to be proud of. The antique, the monuments and even the basic three arts and art of living is not alien to us. It is true that the physical assets, we miss. Please realize the fact that the genes are still with us. Those are assets and we can rejuvenate them in the market. Those are worth for investments. New values and wealth can be created in our local area if we realize and deploy them. It's your factor of production the Almighty have inserted in you. Realize and discover. It is our great culture. Often, it is also an invisible one. But you are smart. You can realize your own strength. If you realize the empty space, in you, wanting to be filled, jump into action. Don't loose time. Your space itself can get vanished. The market is under fast change. You have to be with it for success and to ensure future history.

If we make an attempt to quantify the possession of us, the majority with no history vi-a-viz with the powerful with history, we may realize the fact that most of the factors of production are owned, and managed by them the minority, the powerful and we own the invisible, the much valued patriotic fervour, truth, non-possession, virtues and even lessons on salvation. We, the poor are more philosophic, better nature friendly, environment concerned and even godly. We are proud possessors of all virtues and believe on theory of 'wantlessness'. Whether these are saleable in your nearby market? You should explore? In the market, it's time for us to realize the bitter truth. In the new order, we should concentrate more on saleable to make history. I could so far see in the market only agricultural produce, industrial products and various services with price tags. The truth in the above mentioned proud possession of the majority is not currently saleable. We need not be proud of our possessions having no market.

A realization on our current possessions may be helpful for us to be better market friendly. From the wage we get, both the market and the government pocket the lions' share. Through loans and pledges, we make a shelter to pay off the life and realize the fact that both the shelter and sheltered are worn out and leaving sizable outstanding indebtedness to the inheritor. That is history; history of the large majority of wage earners. We are still sucked by the powerful. Keep your B.P. low and keep out your wild traits for physical fight. Conserve energy and penetrate to the market around. Realize your own strength, save energy and sell your produces, products and services. You have to make a variety of innovations to be successful in the market. You are capable for the same. Your own people make the crowd and new trends will pick up. Make use of them. They can be located more around traditional places. Those are large markets. Providing toilet for them is also a business. Go there, stand alone and observe. Bring to the market, your saleable and express all your suppressed feelings and emotion on selling them; and, making history of yours, not of the Gods there. Realize the fact that the powerful sold even the Gods; and, both the market and its infrastructure are still owned by them. You are a new entry, and therefore, always make use of your brain. It is there in your skull. Rub it and activate. That is self-realization of your own assets. It will help you to be in history.

9.3 *Re-engineering*

Re-engineering is nothing but revitalizing your dead engine by you, the engineer. In the present context, it is mostly idle, or less used by the majority, those having no history. But their batteries can be recharged and the system activated for market friendly operations to make their own humble history. It is a private affair. Under globalization and liberalization, making once own history is market friendly. It can be through re-engineering process as there is no money to buy new engines, new brain and install a new one paying the super specialist doctors on brain transplantation. Let them make use of their gunny pigs. Let us keep away from them and focus on re-engineering of our own brain, owned, possessed and kept presently idle; and therefore, with hidden vast potential.

Recognize the fact that you have brain and it can be activated through your own re-engineering. We have Independence Day, Mother's Day, Teachers Day, Valentine's Day etc. We are yet to think of a Brain Day. Let us initiate to realize ourselves the very fact that all of us possess brain and we are also the blessed. Almighty never produce even one without a head. In films the brainy through their graphics make even headless heroes dance to win the heart of heroines. For entertaining us, they use their heads and thereby they make us aware of our brain. Can you imagine our friends moving in malls headless! It is fun. But how many of them really use their mighty brain power is a subject worth for studies. If not, it is time to address on our vital part. The very touch on it will make your brain tickle and it will be vibrant. We are familiar with the new market. The entry to them can be better possible for us using our own brain. For a buyer, the bulk of his purse is enough. For a market player, innovation is important and it is possible through right re-engineering using our brain. So, you start recognizing, re-engineering the vital part of yours and innovating action for market entry. You are capable and show your merits in the emerging markets. You will make your own history. Don't hesitate. Perform and perfect your dreams and translate your vision through action. That is re-engineering. First you initiate and then stimulate those within your family. The process will ensure your entry into the market, the new order where you can make your fortune and history.

To initiate the re-engineering process, close all books before you and unlearn. Focus on your brain and find new space for your own creative thinking and action points for market intervention. This is easy, as you have less history; and therefore, left with more space to accommodate what is your own. Make an attempt to find what is your own and enlist. Focus on your traits and build your team to address. This itself is the mighty task on re-engineering. Currently, it remains not addressed or less addressed. You constitute the majority and any re-engineering process you initiate will trigger demand and open up new market. Forget the old tags on you. If possible, collect and sell them. Make new tags and hang on your items and sell. Innovate even on tags and win the market. That is history making.

New faculty on management will emerge in you and you will get yourself seasoned in the market as a market player, and not as the familiar consumer. Ward off those hesitate to be with you. They will eat away your time; one of major factors of productions you currently possess. Right from the beginning of the re-engineering process, given top priority to attain higher efficiency. Learn the art from the nearby. If required, even make use of the pavements. If you can't sell, at your place, be mobile. You don't have history and can be vibrant like Michael Jackson. Rehearse at home and perfect yourself and dance to the tune of the market. Never miss the bus. You will be out as happened early. If you have still doubts, try to recollect your own forefathers at least their names. If you are a wage earner, you are the best to address re-engineering. Look into your own services and the methods of your own boss or the government, your invisible boss. Both are currently using you. But, find out the real fact that even your boss is not using you fully. If you find a space within you, you are successful to address the art of re-engineering and reaching higher level in your productive efficiency. Pick up an activity or product required by the market. Focus and perform. If your near and dear are within your boat, you are the blessed. Definitely you will strike the success and make history. When you fly on your own wings, say goodbye to your boss. Never ditch your boss. But use him. That is not sin. It's re-engineering to make you fit into the new order.

Be corporate like. You and your team should have clear vision, mission, strategy, action points, self-monitoring, internalizing, rectifications, optimizing efficiency, perfecting your produce, products, service and making them market friendly. Right from the waste you see in front of your house, anything on your reach, you can focus; and, showcase in the market. Use the social media to shape, perfect and widen the market. New faculty on re-engineering will emerge in you from your action, the surroundings and from the market. You will emerge with added skill; and, that will empower you and your team. This is not in the current schools of management designed by the minority for their performance. Don't waste time on referring or searching to find solutions of your issues or market hurdles. It is a new subject and you have to evolve. You will empower yourself when you initiate. Recognize your brain. Give a chance to it to innovate. It's kept idle for the last 1000 years. Why don't you realize and release the brain power and enable it to re-engineer yourself? Our earlier Teachers never taught us to keep it idle. Then why it is enslaved under the wrong teachings happened during the past few centuries? Break your own chains and allow your own BRAIN to address the mighty re-engineering process to make your own history. Service rules and regulations are for the boss to nurse his culture. When you break them, it is re-engineering for better survival and to make your history. It's a *Sathkarma, a Punya* or a good deed.

Massive social re-engineering Governments initiated mostly yielded poor results. Those are of different models and you need not refer to them and waste your time, energy and increase your B.P. Minority led initiatives are for them, by them and to suck the majority; those with no history.

With alum, you can't address re-engineering. By mistake, it might have stimulated a few of you. Those they flash as success stories and continue their business at your cost. There are a few exceptional volunteer workers and agencies. Let us salute them. They are role models. But your initiatives will trigger an added and massive process. If the successful among the majority help the next neighbour to address his own re-engineering process, the cumulative effect will speed up our efforts on making history. It will also help you to have better daughter-in-law's and son-in-law's as I highlighted earlier.

Look at the above process as an investment. If you are progressive, you look for a better or an equal match to bring in at home as your daughter-in-law. This is possible only when you have availability within your reach and belonging to your favourite culture. So, handhold and help at least one in your neighbourhood to address his own re-engineering. It will enable them to get enlisted in the history and ensure the supply of your likely daughter-in-law or son-in-law. The mighty change you can achieve within your life time and be a history maker. You will have a better expiry with history. It is possible with the simple process of addressing re-engineering yourself and helping a chosen one to address the subject to ensure the supply source to the incoming family members.

The enhanced supply source will also make wider access to market for selectivity. Don't nurse the dream of selecting from the minority. They have made their own history for the past 1000 years and their citadel is impenetrable. Even if you make initial success; you will be in the long run rejected and feel like waste without history. Rather, focus on your own merit. It is worth, saleable and dynamic to your change process. Your market is of the majority. Why do you want to get into a group which you don't belong to? There is no short cut to be in history. We have to make history ourselves. For this purpose, there is a need for re-engineering our own genes to perform in the new market operations. If you can make it a massive program, future history is yours.

Most of our existing institutions, were we have new entry is owned by the minority and led by their paid teachers to keep us in our primitive or earlier status for continuous exploitation. They, therefore, has to tie us with the old threads for their convenience and business. Under this tradition, we will feel ourselves inferior and make us mentally guilty, sick and physically weak. This is cleverly traded and used for trapping the majority and keeping them under their feet.

A re-engineering process perhaps will not be accepted easily by those at home. Smile at them; and, you do your work. You can't change them. Their mind, body and your money they love to surrender to their masters, the minority, the powerful and the ruling class. Realize the fact. That is the merit of their re-engineering initiated just a millennium year back and you and I were used to make their history, the present history and even tuned to make their future history.

Episode 10

Appreciation, Projection and Internalization

10.1 Appreciation

Appreciation is a trait of all living. And, we all love and long for getting appreciated. But we, the majority, somehow are shy on expressing it. We, often fail to observe and appreciate even ourselves. Our trait we use to appreciate the minority, the powerful and those who even made our life miserable in the recent past. It is a strange faculty of ours. Most of us find less scope and fewer items in ourselves and at home worth appreciating. The problem is that even for appreciation; we are habituated to think of others, not of our own. Such trait of ours, need changes. Let us realize ourselves, our existence, our existence as majority and it is worth appreciable and showcasing.

Our faculty of appreciation perhaps is currently tuned to respond on stimulation, on others possessions and power. Often, we spend our energy to degrade our own merits. We are very good at this art; especially those not engaged on productive work and having enough spare time. Market operators are familiar on our traits. And, they exploit the same by pushing in their products and services especially through cable. Earlier, it was done through magazines through never ending stories. Such literature and T.V. serials made history stretching our imagination for decades. Those products were saleable and we the majority paid and nursed the market. The faculty on appreciation and its skill though we had over time, for reasons best known to ourselves, we are hesitant to deploy them for making our own history.

The attitude of negative appreciation had done and is doing large damage to ourselves and our near and dear. Realize the bitter truth, owned and daily practiced by us. We are, somehow destined to spend our scarce energy and time on the subject. Then why can't we channel it to the faculty of positive appreciation? Just change; and plug it, in the desired slot. We all will be happy; and we can also play better in market. Realize the fact that it is a valuable trait, and it can be used as a new factor of production, especially to make an entry in the fast growing service sector. You can make money and open your account in history. A change in our mind set in favour of positive appreciation of our own near and dear will open new avenues like the mighty sun break open the darkness. The break is possible only when we address the subject first ourselves.

To begin with, we should have a faculty to appreciate ourselves. Our qualities worth marketing must be traced, found out or discovered. A self-search will enable us to have the much-wanted triggering effect. If we fail to appreciate ourselves, who will appreciate us? The urge for getting appreciated is within. We can't sweep out our own urge waiting for centuries. So, let us start pressing on, like the much familiar handset or cell phone at hand. Use the surfing faculty we got currently through our handset. No extra expenditure. Surf on to yourself; your family members and surf on the neighbourhood worth appreciation. Like Columbus and Vas-co-Da-Gama, you will find a spectrum of your own new world worth appreciating, recording, showcasing and history making. Can we call it as value addition? Please search and find out. If positive, flash the signals and institutionalize. That is part of your future history.

We the elders grew up hearing progressively shorter stories on us and our family. We can't blame our parents. They too heard less or nothing of theirs. Rather they were on the run for their life. Perhaps, you may appreciate our genes on fear, deprivation, hunger, lifesaving skill, immense patience on sustenance and suppressed feelings on mutual hate, lack of faith and even fear to express love. It all happened due to our own rich past, the great culture, we appreciate. Time has changed. You are not compelled to beat on the same drum and chant on your rich past. Live for your life at present. Discover yourself and appreciate. The paradise is right in front and at your reach. Start appreciating your body, mind and soul and your own near and dear and your own emotions and enjoy. In place of fear, neglect and mistrust, fill in the space with new faculty on appreciations. Trace and find the hidden genes in you and never wait for others appreciation, especially from the minority, the present market players. They knew where your bullocks and your carts are and will kick and divert you; out from history. Watch out and perform. Keep in mind the electric fluctuations at home and the role of stabilizer. Learn the habit of tuning up and tuning down to avoid the likely shock. But tune on. We need faculty of appreciation to make history.

Our own great culture planted hatred within us. Invaders were also equally cruel and rude to us. Incidentally, they taught a few lessons to enable us to appreciate ourselves. Only the minority among us picked up the threads. There again, we missed the opportunity to address the subject. In the present scenario, our fellowmen are more market centric. It is right time, we start appreciating our own merits and showcase our own saleable and face the competition, survive and flourish in the market to make history. Otherwise, we will get deleted as earlier even from the forthcoming history. You will have no role in the next future film or tear jerking serials right at home. Never join in a queue of a ration shop or beverage outlet. Those are alms rationed out by the govt: to create beggars to keep them alive and to delete after voting. The culture is currently celebrated by us, the history less. Beggars can't make history. Jump the queue and make history. You're born not to stand in a queue. To look at you and appreciate yourself, you need not fear or spend money. But, you should have the proud will. The much required will to change and create history. Or eat mud. It's not new to us. Even our Teachers were once forced to eat hard mud. And, a few of us were used for the dirty deed. If you're unaware, that itself is the reason why you and I are currently not in history. Come out of the trap; perform and capture future history. It's yours. Learn to appreciate the better quality gene in you. Never join the queue designed by the powerful. It is the place they use to exhibit you as a beggar. You have a market value and learn to appreciate yourself. That will lead your clan to history.

Beware; we carry a lot of dirty genes with us. That is why we still love negative marketing. Films we viewed earlier in theatres were 3 hours plus length. Similar to that, the time for our extraction and further termination was bit extended during our early days. Now, in the present market, with a scratch on our purse, we can be drained and made bankrupt. The history less or those with shorter history are like the shorter film we see, of late. The shortest in real life is suicide. And, by adopting the method, the majority, the history less, is making history by making the media record their own shortest history. An easy way to reach the Almighty is wrongly understood and practiced. For the media, it is a growing business. They hunt for them. daily. We the majority, unfortunately ensure the supply. We create a new market, awaiting fast growth and nurturing scope for emerging another *avatar* to address the menace. Though we don't have history, it appears that we are good at creating future gods to repeat the past trends in history. Stop the drama; and focus on market for making your own history. Appreciate the self in you and learn to buy the essentials from the emerging market and never stand on a queue even for a bottle of beer. By doing it you're keeping your neck on the Gallatin designed by the power wielding butchers for your own killing. As a history maker, realize the trap and jump out from the queue. Unfortunately, it is the most pathetic scene on the side of the roads on 21 Century. It reflexes our rulers dirty mind to trap the majority under perpetual slavery. Open up your mind, realize and appreciate yourself and attribute values for yourself. Get out of the trap. You are at history making.

The faculty of appreciation, positive appreciation, has to be carefully nursed in our own gene. Let us be aware of the fact, and attempt. Keep away those who stick to their old practices and those who hesitate to change. You will find them at home. Carry them on your shoulders like the cross Jesus loved to carry for us. If you are tired, keep them down and proceed. You are not Jesus to carry that burden for ever. You too, need a familiar break. Your burdens are more environment friendly. They can relax at the river banks, look at the stars, quench their thrust and get themselves dissolved, better organic; and not leaving a trace in history. But, you are different. You love to make history; and therefore, start appreciating first yourself. It is not in scriptures. Markets are the current reality where you have to find your place to make history. Your success stories will shape new ethics 'new scriptures' fit for your time. You are familiar with cycling. Continue cycling appreciating at least yourself. You will be in history.

Realize the fact that we are in the market. More time we spend on market operations. Farmers among us have long history on their profession and they too, of late, look in to the market before taking decision on farm operations.

Appreciation of the market and its dynamic status, we learn on a daily basis. The smart among us, even refer to the index on stock market. Large ad: columns on sky scrapers, we see on our ad-papers daily morning with wide open eyes and even wider mouth. We appreciate the full front page on advertisements and of late, developed patience to search for top news on subsequent pages. It is a changing process on our appreciation. Make use of the already changed process in your favour. We are not in history, because we were not with the changing world. Be with the wind; appreciate changes and fly. Through the faculty on appreciation, you can flood the market with your own stuff. By appreciating your own people, you can break the strong citadels on advertisements. 'It is easy to read'. Also, realize the fact that it is difficult to break the thread the minority, the powerful, bounded on us. We are still slave like. Realize. If any doubt, break, showcase and appreciate. Take it as challenge. You can make your history, if you can develop a faculty on appreciation. It will take you to the market and empower you to excel and lead you to your own appreciable future history.

By triggering self-appreciation, we can have better access to our own strength to get into the market. Even today, we are sizable minor players in them. We are the sources of supply of the essentials and the manpower and its varied skill. Realize the fact that we currently ensure the supply as per the guidance of the minority, the powerful having history. Realization of this larger truth will empower us in innovative market intervention. The old cartels and other market mechanisms are known to us. But, we are yet to make use of them for our own benefits and therefore, we still remain the large set of people without history. The present generation is better market savvy and we parents should not scare them with our old stories and myth. Let us close our rooms and silently pray for them. When out of our room, if possible, handhold them in their venture. If you have the skill, guide them to sell in the market and enable your ward to make money, make history. Don't stand folding your hand criticizing or wondering. Never put a coin earned by them in the loft or Hundy kept by the powerful in which you have no stake. Appreciate your own old faculty and search out coins from your own purse and fill those coffers. Leave the youth to make their own history.

We elders should realize the fact that we are the major hurdles at home preventing our children's' growth in the market. I salute you for bringing up the young. But, I also plea to desist from the practice of holding them off from market led operations. Realize the fact that we were used and thrown out by the minority when we missed our bus. There is nothing to be proud to ward off kids inducing fear and reminding the unfortunate age old practices. Let us make them free. You enjoy watching their performance and if possible, handhold them. That is the only way to mend up the lost time and to regain the lost status. Remember, the degradation was at work for over 1000 years. More than 30 generations we underwent value degradation and that made us not in history. Let us not repeat the same mistake; especially when we are on the subject of making our own history. In the place of historical and cultural revolutions, market operations has become the vehicle of change. Appreciate the changes and be inclusive to make future history. Get into the new Bus. Innovate and appreciate.

Also realize the fact that the genes in you and me is misled in the past, over 1000 years and it needs rejuvenation. In the great melee, the genes within us was forced by fear to sleep;

and that made us timid and shy. If left unchecked, the status will continue and we will force our children again outcaste from history. Realize the fact that you are destined to throttle your own kids due to ignorance induced in you as proud culture. If you have doubts, search within your own house. You can see symptoms of fear and strings on innumerable bonds on slavery. Realize the fact that even today we wrongly continue to plant fear in our own kids. How can they create history when they are in fear? Let us own our mistake and desist from the millennium old wrong practices, not allowing our own children even to express their liking at home. This culture has to be changed, especially when you are market savvy and love to be in history. Appreciate the fact that our faculty on appreciation need tuning up. Internalize the same and address re-engineering first within you and at home. Your actions will snow ball to the much desired synergy to make history of yours.

10.2 *Projection*

Projection! Projection of What?

Yourself! Your kith and kin!

If we can't do it, who will do for us? The subject of projection, especially self-projection is Greek and Latin to us, the majority. Instead, we have a great shy on our self-projection. We are more natural (wild) and spiritual being a mediocre. The truth may be we are less cunning, more timid and therefore, we love to project others; especially those Hollywood, Bollywood heroes and heroines, politicians and even the corrupt. They are bold and beautiful and sexy for us. We all love them and also find time and space to project them. In traffic signals, through larger flexes and hoardings and through cables they live with us even in our dreams. It is our culture, and often we are proud of our own culture. The guy having shyness to look at his own body likes to affix a blow-up of his favourite in his room. It's a style, a shameless style happens due to his timidity. The culture is made public through films and through cables and the minority make money. Still we hesitate to look at ourselves and project. We are yet to start loving ourselves and those at home. Remove such posters at home and affix yours. Remains of such posters, if found in future excavations, may force the researchers to draw wrong inference like existence of studs and fake heroes reach Godly status

We are notorious in our skill in history making. Please don't provide opportunity for such conclusions. You make your history by fixing your blow up at home. It's very cheap now in the market. Your great grandchildren will grow up realizing their true history. Projecting yourself is not sin. It's marketing in the new era of globalization. Please remove all those wrong blow-ups and install yours and project. That is history making.

We don't love to project or talk about our own family and our history. But, we know a few generations of our own leaders and heroes even though they are yet to recognize our existence. We love projecting others; and if possible, reversing the process to our own. While doing the same, we feel like possessed by spirits, the devils within us and who rule us. We still love to be with the mud and slush, more down to earth or even beneath the earth - the much familiar locations where Dracula relaxed and rose to suck blood. We don't love to dig to find our old skeletons. We don't like the foul smell and their horrible appearance. This happens due to our own false prestige or ignorance. There is nothing to be proud of it. The much inherited shame of ours should be rather shed and the energy diverted to project our own merits. If found incapable, at least project your own children's achievements and handhold them to be in the market. Parents can't be younger than their own kids. They would age out and leave without history, if unable to project. Desist from the inherited trait to shoot missiles down to the mud keeping your kids at its tip. Sky is up there. You look above. Your neck will not cramp. Shoot them up towards the sky. You please showcase the process and the energy as the missile scientist the Honourable President of India had shown to you. You will be enlisted in history, by our own kids, the history makers.

Not just once, but for a long time, we were taught not to project. Projection was even punishable. We were a disciplined lot; lost in myth, the powerful created. It was implanted in our genes and we were taught to be proud to be in mud and seek salvation over a period of their choice, extending to generations. Now, we are liberated under market mechanism. Still majority of us like to live in mud. It is perhaps due to a curse on us for our earlier deeds in stamping our own Teachers who worked for our empowerment; and, we based on the orders given by the minority, the powerful, stamped them, our own Gurus, with our own foot under the mud. The faculty of projection perhaps thereby dried and waned out in our genes due to our own guilty conscious. The minority, the powerful, are never burdened with such curse. They never did it. We only did it; and, it is time to realize, repent and resurrect. If any of your kid is showing the guts on resurrection, keep away from them. Or, you will be nowhere in history. Like our ignorant forefathers, leaving no history, we too will exit similar to a bubble on the muddy water.

To project ourselves, shed the inherent shyness. There is no beauty in it. We were wrongly taught on it especially to our own females to always hide them in shyness. Of late, our women are getting out of the stamp of shyness on them. Yet, they look beautiful and climb the ladder like world beauties contest, take up the role of proud motherhood, better lovers and the loved, projecting themselves. They appear much faster and result oriented in projecting themselves compared to our male. Men, take their own time to shed shyness. As a result, they are likely to fall behind our women to make new trends in market. It is creating new space in market in favour of woman. Make use of the opportunity and create history.

We should tune up our own genes and project ourselves. Nature has designed us to project and compete. Market is the new avenue. Project yourself and invade. The gene is inherent. Be aggressive and inroad in the universal market. Make history, your own records on your achievements using even innovative instruments on projection. Institutionalize projection. Steal the show. You lose only your shame. But, you will make history. Try to project your near and dear at home. Replace the wall hangings with new blow up, photographs, painting and other creative work of your own people at home. Use your own canvass and don't allow others to sit on your chest and make their history. It's wrong projection. Earlier it was called slavery. Come out of the great trap and make your history, project yourself and your family.

The clever had perched their tents even in our homes. There is less space at home and even in our hearts. There can be resistance, due to convention. Don't care. Throw them out and decorate the walls and courtyard with your own history.

If possible, grab the opportunities even in neighbourhood. Name the streets, if they are unnamed. Establish utility centres in your name, if you are a history maker; and, in the names of the successful change agents around you. Project the locally available performers and those of the flora and fauna of Mother Nature, and hidden there. It will project your local area and promote tourism in your place. Develop a faculty to be cool to the likely resistance on projection. A friend of mine located a beautiful face of his wife in her XIIth class group photo. With the help of a portrait painter, blew up and hung on wall. Looking at the painting, his elderly wife could see her ghost in it. The house turned haunted. He was unhappy. I share the incident to enable you watch out. When you start projecting yourself, even ghost can emerge at home. Be careful. But carry on with your projection to be in history. Ghosts are with us for the last one millennium. Let us project ourselves and eject out the ghost within us.

For projecting yourselves, you can be better innovative at home where you are the master. If you fall back on the familiar tools and methods, you may find difficulty in breaking the ice, creating history and conquering the market. Invent new methods and models to project. Experiment at home and showcase perfected products and services in the market and make history. Your tools on projection should be user friendly and appealing to the market. Right from personality projection like a good haircut, innovation on facial appearance, dress codes, footwear, umbrella, toys, baby care, night dress, occasion and vocation wears, aroma clothes, baby care products, pre and post-natal care products, requirement of the elders, teenagers, the local area bold and beautiful, equipment's required for education, skill formation, medical and healthcare etc. you may scan and select for projection at home, perfect and emerge in the market. Your own home can be your lab or workshop on projection. If you initiate, others will follow, especially your own kids, the prospective history makers. Also, invest in tools and equipment fit for projecting even the dead at home. You can make history in the market, selling your new tool kits, services and showcasing those specimens traditionally possessed and having skill to see ghost within, and sell to the forthcoming students, interested in history. If someone can sell Dracula, why the majority hesitate to sell our own ghosts? Patent them. Now local area or even family based claims may be possible. But project them. Be inclusive. Don't miss the opportunity.

If you initiate, others, especially your neighbour will also join. Project upward and you will be enlightened. The process is worth celebration like *Diwali* festival in India when all lit their lamps and compete to light maximum number of lamps forgetting the enlightenment day of the great teachers who once empowered us to witness the switch over from Dark to the Light, the enlightenment; and, we chose the Dark. While projecting, take care of the past strings. If you find them in the new light you lit, burn them. It will enable you to be in your new action on projection of you, your family, your products and services. The added faculty in projection will take you to higher levels of love, care and compassion. Your life you will feel worth living and an internal urge on history making will guide you to conquest new realms in market.

Be market friendly. I repeat. Mould your saleable for the market in your local area. Your experience will emerge as the new history. It will open new platforms for all your loved one to perform. Know your own strength in market manipulation. Make a banging sound, using your steel plate and spoon at home. You can throw out from the market even the mighty. If you are shy to make use of steel plate and spoon, make use of your handset, your cell phone, and be viral like the real virus that terrorized you in history and swept out many of our forefathers. Be aggressive and inroad in to the market and project. You can do it. Your body chemistry can realize the fact that time immemorial you lived without history and it is time to make your mark through the market mechanism. Realize your opportunity and your strength. You belong to the majority, the sizable. Don't behave like elephants; to be led by the small perched on top of it. Be smart. Project yourself and be in history. Leave something for your kids. Don't throw them to the boiling oil. You should feel proud to switch over to the market mechanism projecting your own achievements. If you feel you have nothing to project, be bold to sell even your primitive history. That will take care of your interest to make history.

10.3 *Internalization*

I am selfish and to the core. I could break the shame in me and through the pretext of handholding; I'm making an entry to the market. My product is the present book you read. If you make an attempt to make history, my market will shrink in the long run. If not, my market will pick up. We have history of throwing away our teachers. I would love to be in their team and making history, everlasting history. You may feel, I'm using you. If you are realizing the truth, your body chemistry is at work. With simple tactics and cock and bull stories, the powerful could keep us in dark without history over a millennium. That is history, our unwritten true history. We are the vast set of unacknowledged, the set being sucked in real history.

If we don't have a child, we should produce one. If any problem, seek medical aid. If we don't have a house, we make one. If incapable, live on streets or in slums. Similarly, if we don't have history, make our own history. Our children will have history; their own history. They need not run behind the excavators. It can be made available in electronic gadgets familiar to them. It is a large business. Of late, a few clever among us are on market with the history of the bride and bridegroom in marriage and related functions. It is a tip of the vast potential market. If you can innovate, you can be a major player in handholding the prospective history makers. There is an increasing urge among the majority to have history of their own and it will open up large scope for business. Make use of the same and make history, also make money. Of late, that is history making. If you have money, you can buy anything including power and history. If you still find yourself in difficulty, open a note book, think, write and attempt to internalize the change you envisage.

The art of history making is subject to your ingenuity. It can be true to the core or spicy as our existing recorded history and thrilling stories in mythology. The creativity in you has freedom to perform, especially when you are making in your history and its non-conventional recording unlike the earlier sculptors and inscription on rocks and metal. Now, the trend is electronic and virulence. You are the masters of your trade, and I'm outdated stamped with expiry date. I reserve my comments and you perform to your best and my blessings for the same. Never forget the fact that history is important. Even Gods have history. Without history, they could never survive. You can attempt a census survey on the subject, if interested. In my local area, a few of our Gods were killed before my eyes. Their history is yet to be recorded. It's a fact. I find new scope on tracing their history and making money.

I have travelled through my time more without history. Of late only, I became aware of the very fact that I will close my life not being in history. The worry made me to scribble these notes. If I could handhold you to think and act on the subject, the purpose is half served. If you also could handhold another to replicate, then the desired institutionalization will set in. Ultimately, it should emerge as a culture. Those having a history of their own should be proud of it. Others canvas can be even empty. Never get dejected. Make use of the opportunity and fill in. Your daily diary can be a history note for the incoming generations. Use the electronic gadgets to record data and information; about you and your family and neighbourhood. Draw professionals' help to showcase at home and even to display in the market. Explore market potentials on the subject. Internalize the culture and institutionalize. Let us leave, leaving something for our nearest. Even the great conquerors left open hand. That is history of the powerful; and we are forced to read them even today. I am talking on a new subject – our history – the history of the vast majority, who currently don't have any history.

The book is a beginning on the large work. Much remains to be done. Plug in and perform. You will feel proud and enlightened in the journey of making your future history.

This book will be available on the below websites

www.ingramcontent.com/pod-product-compliance
Lightning Source LLC
Chambersburg PA
CBHW051447250726
48655CB00001B/279